NEW WELSH REVIEW

With thanks to Gwen Davies

The team at Parthian and the *New Welsh Review* would like to thank Gwen Davies for her innovative and engaged editorship of the *New Welsh Review* over more than a decade.

Susie Wild has been appointed as the editor. Her first issue, 138 Summer 25, will be published in June with design by Olwen Fowler. It will feature new work by among others Philip Gross and clare e potter.

Please see inside back cover for more details.

New Welsh Review
The Old Surgery
Cardigan SA43 1ED

www.newwelshreview.com

New Welsh Review was established in 1988 by Academi and the Association for Welsh Writing in English.

Editor:
Gwen Davies
editor.newwelshreview@gmail.com

Management Board:
David Lloyd-Owen, Niall Griffiths and Richard Davies

Patrons:
Richard S Powell and Bob Borzello

Design:
Ingleby Davies Design and Syncopated Pandemonium

Proofreading:
Steven Lovatt

Cover image: Cover Art: Isabel Alexander. Tom Evans [TE], 1944, lithograph, 37 x 27cm. ; image on contents page: 'Mari Lwyd Chat', William McClure Brown, courtesy of artist's estate and School of Art Museums and Galleries, Aberystwyth University.

The contents: © The New Welsh Review Ltd and the authors

Print ISBN: 978-1-913830-30-4
eBook ISBN: 978-1-913830-31-1
ISSN: 09542116

ARTIST STORY:
LEARNING TO FLY

KATARINA KRIŠTÚFKOVÁ ON HER PHOTOGRAPHY
TRANSLATED BY **JULIA SHERWOOD**

MY HUSBAND DIDN'T LIKE FLYING.

I, on the other hand, have always been fascinated by the way airports are organised and the physical miracle that allows bodies of such huge weight to stay up in the air.

My husband's untimely tragic death plunged me into darkness. For months, I wandered around, utterly lost.

Sometimes it would bring me relief to look up. Towards the sun, the clouds... and the aeroplanes, so easily crossing our earthly borders, closed by Covid.

And all of a sudden, the light that had been extinguished inside me was lit up again by the thought that I, too, could learn to fly.

My photo of aeroplanes was taken in the hangar of a small airfield, where my flying school is based. These are the planes in which I learned how to fly... and live again.

Photographer **Katarina Krištúfková** is a project manager at Film Europe SK. She lives in Bratislava and is the widow of author and screenwriter Peter Krištúfek, who sadly died in 2018 at the age of forty-four (a tribute to him, 'Seminars in Gastronomy and Abandoned Gardens' by Dado Nagy is in these pages).

pp 4–5: 'Boy on Bicycle'
p 6: 'Aeroplanes', both photographs by Katarína Krištúfková

Where will your reading take you next?

From Rio to Ramallah, Tbilisi to Tokyo, explore cities the world over through the eyes of their authors with Comma Press' 'Reading the City' series.

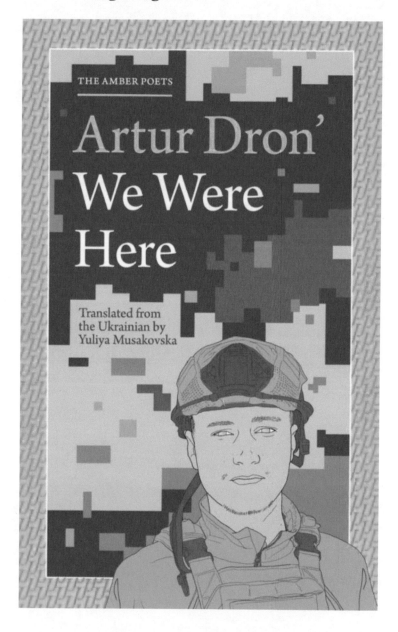

THE AMBER POETS

Artur Dron'
We Were
Here

Translated from
the Ukrainian by
Yuliya Musakovska

FROM OBSCURITY TO A PLACE ON THE MAP OF WORLD LITERATURE

JULIA SHERWOOD ON SLOVAK LITERATURE IN ENGLISH TRANSLATION

SLOVAK LITERATURE LONG REMAINED VIRTUALLY UNKNOWN OUTSIDE its homeland. The editors of the late Victorian-era compilation of world literature, *The Universal Anthology* (1899) gave the following assessment:

> In the short time of its existence, their literature has produced some remarkable productions, that compare favourably with those of more fortunate and larger nations. Having no national existence, and suffering from the oppression of the Hungarians, much of their literature is a lament and a dirge. But of late they are taking a broader aspect of life, though they prefer mainly to use national themes for literary purposes.

Although things changed for the better after 1918, when Slovakia became (the smaller) part of the newly formed country of Czechoslovakia, the work of Slovak writers remained in the shadow of their neighbours, particularly their Czech compatriots throughout most of the twentieth century. It was not until 1987 that the first-ever conference devoted specifically to Slovak literature in the second half of the last century was organised by Robert Pynsent, one of its few champions in the UK, who noted in his introduction to the collection of conference papers, *Modern Slovak Prose* (1990), that it was 'the Slovak language that has hitherto kept most scholars and readers in the West ignorant of Slovak literature. Slovak writers are translated into other socialist-bloc languages, but even that does not mean that they are widely read [...] Slovak literature has not grown in isolation, but a certain isolation has been imposed on Slovak literature.'

That isolation was most acute in terms of reaching English-language readers, but in the new millennium we have seen quite a dramatic change of fortune. Many works of Slovak literature are now available in English, despite the anglophone market's notorious resistance to translation, compounded by the decline in language teaching in UK primary and secondary schools and the closure or decimation of language and literature departments at British universities.

Fifteen years ago, when I started out as a translator, few publishers were willing to take on unknown authors from a small Central European country. But since then, largely thanks to translation grants provided by funding bodies in Slovakia – the SLOLIA grant scheme and Slovak Arts Council (FPU) grants deserve special praise – several publishers in the UK have been able to take the leap and give hitherto unknown writers from this relatively little-known country a chance, and my husband Peter Sherwood and I have been among those fortunate to act as conduits on this journey.

Slovak literature has also enjoyed the support of the European Literature Network, and works by Slovak writers have been published in such acclaimed journals as *Two Lines*, *Words Without Borders* and *Asymptote*.

Overall, in the thirty years from 1989 to 2019, no less than 62 books by Slovak writers (prose, poetry and anthologies) have appeared in English. While some years were better than others, the average was two books per year. By comparison, between 2020 and 2024 the yearly average more than doubled to 4.8, with twenty-four books by Slovak writers published in English over these five years. 2024 was one of the best, with six publications, and 2025 is shaping up to be a bumper year, with at least ten books by Slovak writers in the offing.

Most of these books were published by smaller, independent houses that are not primarily profit-oriented: trailblazing work was done by Garnett Press, who published four books by Slovak writers, followed by Jantar Publishing and Parthian Books, who have consistently championed Slovak

- ## 2024: Slovak books in English

  - ### 7 authors

    Balla, Katarína Kucbelová, Ivan Lesay, Peter Macsovszky, Dušan Mitana, Peter Milčák, Ján Rozner

  - ### 6 translators

    Jonathan Gresty, John Minahane, Magdalena Mullek, Julia and Peter Sherwood, David Short

  - ### 5 publishers

    Guernica Press, Jantar Publishing, Karolinum Press, Modrý Peter/Fooliar Press, Seagull Books

Slovak books in English translation published during 2024.

literature, with eight and six books respectively by Slovak writers under their belt. And more recently, two new players have emerged: firstly, the Calcutta-based Seagull Books, whose Slovak list, launched in 2022, has clocked up nine books by Slovak authors to date, while in 2023, Karolinum Press in Prague launched their Modern Slovak Classics series, which has seen two books published, with four more in the works.

This positive trend is reflected in a new collection of essays on Slovak literature, *Home and the World in Slovak Writing. A Small Nation's Literature in Context* (McGill–Queen's University Press, March 2025), edited by Katarína Gephardt, Ivana Taranenková and Charles Sabatos, with contributions from nine highly respected Slovak literature specialists. In his foreword to the collection, McGill University literature scholar, Daniel W Pratt, writes:

> Slovak literature has transformed from a hidden gem to a rich and stable tradition in the centre of Europe. Perhaps most remarkably, Slovak literature is hitting a high mark domestically at the same time as a group of talented and dedicated translators are exposing the rest of the world to it. Slovak literature is being translated primarily into the languages of their neighbours, ie German, Czech, Hungarian, and Polish, but the new English-language versions show a burgeoning wider reach. The English-speaking world can access some of the latest Slovak literature almost simultaneously with its new developments, a true rarity for Central European cultures.

The volume aims to map the key milestones and themes in the development of Slovak literature, focusing on the period from 1989 to the present, and covering pivotal historical moments and literary themes, while highlighting books that have been translated into English.

These include works by Peter Krištúfek and Uršuľa Kovalyk, authors that, notably, Cardigan-based Parthian Books have championed in the English-speaking world over the past ten years. Parthian's latest – Nicol Hochholczerová's ground- and taboo-breaking debut, *This Room Is Impossible To Eat* (to be published in April) – is a major literary achievement that is bound to cement Slovak literature's growing international reputation.

Slovak books in translation published by Parthian.

Julia Sherwood is an award-winning translator and literary organiser. She was born and grew up in Bratislava, and after studying English and Slavonic languages and literature in Cologne, London and Munich she settled in the UK. She is editor-at-large representing Slovakia for the online literary journal, *Asymptote*. Julia lives in London with her husband, Peter Sherwood, a linguist and translator, with whom she has published many translations, including *This Room Is Impossible To Eat.*

We interview Nicol Hochholczerová in these pages about her novella, This Room Is Impossible To Eat.

Photo: Marek Šulík

SEMINARS IN GASTRONOMY AND ABANDONED GARDENS

DADO NAGY ON HIS FRIENDSHIP WITH THE LATE PETER KRIŠTÚFEK
TRANSLATED FROM THE SLOVAK BY **JULIA SHERWOOD**

To WRITE ABOUT PETER MEANS TO ME, FIRST AND FOREMOST, TO TELL the story of our friendship. Apart from hanging out in cafés, we worked together on a number of projects, such as composing film-like dialogues, co-writing a crime story, and TV and radio shows, as well as being involved in a bizarre theatre show at the Black Raven club. Any excuse for a meeting was welcome.

One of the best excuses was what we used to call Seminars in Gastronomy – a contest in inventing dishes that told stories on a given theme. These gatherings for around ten friends plus some additional guests always followed a set structure: tasting, analysing, awarding the prize and chronicling the whole event.

A few more seminars have been held since Peter left us but it just wasn't the same anymore.

My café chinwags with Peter would start in the morning, often extending into lunch and an endless seeing-each-other-home, some train watching and an even more prolonged, zen-like, saying of goodbyes....

In my mind's eye I see Peter's first attempts at directing – the short student films and video clips for his songs in which I would appear playing the part of, for example, the man studying beetles in the botanical garden, the slow-witted son, or one half of a kissing couple passed by a car.

And last but not least, *The Hungarian Dressmaker*, the feature film directed by Iveta Grofová from Peter's novella and script.

Music was another of his gifts. He was a member of Cadillac dei, a band he'd founded with some former schoolmates. They rehearsed regularly and played the odd gig. For, as he used to say, the best thing about playing in a band are the five minutes after the gig.

For the last three years, almost every Monday morning after I deposited my son in nursery school, Peter and I would set out for exploratory walks in our city of Bratislava, especially around the hilly residential area under the Slavín monument. We'd stop for a coffee at the café in the woods at Horský park, before scrambling up Kalvária hill and walking down Hlboká cesta back to the centre of the city.

This being the period when Peter had become completely addicted to collecting old printed matter, I regularly had to fend off his exhortations to force illegal entry into various seemingly abandoned houses in the vicinity. Because you never knew – there may have been some rare books there....

Peter grew up on the Koliba Hill in an old house surrounded by gardens and vineyards. The unique atmosphere of the area forms the backdrop to his poems and stories, such as the tale of the twins who lived across the street; of Mr Slušný, a local brawler; his grandma, a former teacher suffering from memory loss who would run away from home; his eccentric mother Zora, and the night jungle he passed through on his way home after a late night at the radio.

In fact, this world existed mainly in his memory and imagination. To reach those real 'abandoned gardens' we usually had to trudge through endless boring new streets, passing newly built houses behind tall fences.

The first time I realised that Peter was a truly great writer was when I read his short story 'The Man Who Had his Shoes Shined'. It tells the story of the first person to be photographed, by Louis Daguerre in 1838 on a busy Paris boulevard. The man is standing there having his shoes shined, as hundreds of people and carriages streamed past, the only one who stayed in one place for long enough to be captured by a daguerreotype, the precursor of photography, and thus be preserved for eternity.

The work that holds a unique position in Peter's oeuvre is the conceptual book *The Atlas of Forgetting*, which shines a light on the last hundred years of Slovakia's history through documents, both known and unknown.

And then, of course, his great novel, *The House of the Deaf Man*, which resembles, in more ways than one, the Hungarian modernist Péter Esterházy's *Revised Edition*, in the ways in which it exposes skeletons in the cupboard that people would rather not talk about.

Peter embodied a rare combination of vast knowledge, a sense of humour and love of parody, as well as a bohemian and venturesome, single-minded spirit. He had a tremendous sense of responsibility and capacity for hard work. Though an introvert, he would expend a huge amount of energy on cultivating intense friendships with people he felt close to. This is best illustrated by his friendship with the bibliophile and writer Kornel Földvári, forty years his senior, whose memoir Peter decided to compile on the basis of his stories. For several years they would meet every Thursday at the Ex Libris café where Peter recorded hours of Kornel's inexhaustible treasure trove of stories, later sorting, abridging and consolidating one version after another. The editing alone took him about two years.

At the same time, Peter embarked on the mammoth task of tidying up and sorting thematically the gigantic, disorganised mountain of books cluttering Kornel's home. Thanks to Peter, a part of this vast library is on display at the Slovak National Gallery. He brought the same meticulousness and single-mindedness to every one of his projects – be it film or book production or their presentations.

Yes, yes, the world is a beautiful place to be born into....

All of this might give you a hint of what sort of person Peter Krištúfek was. Nevertheless, I realise that... well, actually, I don't know. And that's a good thing.

Some people are much more colourful, complex and mysterious than they appear to be. That is why they write stories. And that is why the only possible way to describe them, while preserving what is truly interesting about them, is through fiction.

Jozef 'Dado' Nagy was born in Bratislava in 1970, and is a Slovakian literary publicist, editor, moderator and propagator of literature. He was a close friend of the late Peter Krištúfek, whose novel *The House of the Deaf Man* (translated by Peter and Julia Sherwood) is forthcoming in a new edition from Parthian.

A film, The Hungarian Dressmaker, *based on Peter Krištúfek's book (*Emma and the Death's Head*) was last year's Slovakia entry to the international feature film category of the 2025 Oscars.*

'I WANTED THOSE FEELINGS PRINTED ON THE PAGE TO BE AS RAW AS POSSIBLE'

IMOGEN DAVIES IN CONVERSATION WITH NICOL HOCHHOLCZEROVÁ
ABOUT THIS ROOM IS IMPOSSIBLE TO EAT

NICOL HOCHHOLCZEROVÁ IS A YOUNG WRITER AND ILLUSTRATOR who grew up in Rimavská Sobota, Slovakia. Originally published in 2021, her book-length debut, *Táto izba sa nedá zjesť* (*This Room Is Impossible to Eat*, forthcoming from Parthian in spring 2025 in a translation by Peter and Julia Sherwood, and extracted in these pages) was shortlisted for Slovakia's most prestigious literary prize, the Anasoft Litera Award, and has since been translated into Bulgarian, Czech, Hungarian, Serbian, Polish and Ukrainian, with German, Macedonian, and French translations underway.

Hochholczerová was named Young Artist of the Year by the Tatra Banka Foundation in 2022, and the following year saw a theatre adaptation of her debut novella at the City Theatre in Žilina. A stage version and a film adaptation are currently being revised in Czech.

In 2024, Hochholczerová completed her Master's in graphic design at the Academy of Art in Banská Bystrica, as well as becoming one of the most talked-about Slovak writers on the European literary scene, due to the controversial nature of her work.

This Room Is Impossible to Eat captures the disturbing progression of a relationship between a twelve-year-old girl (Tereza) and her fifty-year-old art schoolteacher (Ivan). Narrated alternately from the points of view of Tereza and Ivan, we witness how the teacher worms his way into Tereza's consciousness, and the distortions of Ivan's mind that make him succeed in controlling and abusing her. The bitesize chapters are unapologetically raw yet poetic snapshots of a relationship that develops from their first meeting right up to when Tereza becomes an adult at eighteen, and Ivan is well into middle age at fifty-seven years old. Each page leaves a bitter and unforgettable taste in your mouth.

NWR: What literary influences shaped the writing of *This Room is Impossible to Eat*?

NH: By the time I started writing this story, I remember becoming less and less interested in what was happening to characters in the books I was reading. Instead, I wanted to know how they feel when something is happening to them, and I wanted those feelings printed on the pages to be as raw as possible. I remember finding exactly that in the writings of Elfriede Jelinek or Ágota Kristóf, but mostly in Aglaja Veteranyi's *Why the Child is Cooking in the Polenta*. I also recall being captivated by texts in which the emotion was less raw, and it all felt like a hazy dream – those books likely had some kind of a plot, but that specific peculiar feeling is what I remember vividly, years after reading them. The works of Mircea Cărtărescu or Italo Calvino come to mind when I think of this kind of literature. And then there is one particular essay from that time that had a huge influence on me: Rebecca Tamás' *The Songs of Hecate: Poetry and the Language of the Occult*, published in the *White Review*.

NWR: Hungarian fairy tales seem to have made a significant impression on the protagonist. Did any fairytales from your childhood make a lasting impression on you?

NH: Some of my most vivid memories from childhood are connected to Hungarian fairytales. I remember standing on a chair in my grandparents' living room, singing, to their guests, the theme tune of the animated series about King Matthias I [the historical medieval king of Hungary and Croatia, around whom folk-tales circulated]. One time, I even taught myself to walk and move my arms exactly like Mattie the Goose Boy from the 1977 animated version (https://en.wikipedia.org/wiki/Mattie_the_Goose-boy_ (1977_film)) of the Hungarian poem by Mihály Fazekas. I was told I would spend hours watching animated movies until I could recite the dialogue word for word. I believe this played a huge part in my love for writing – often my 'writing' as a child consisted mainly of drawing characters or the world they lived in, an approach akin to concept art for animation. However, I did not, as a nine-year-old, have the skills or resources to create an entire movie, so I stuck to writing and illustration.

So, of course, these fairytales hold a sentimental value for me, but they are also fascinating to watch as an adult, since you notice completely new things. There is this particular fairytale in which a princess asks a swineherd for his three piglets because they can dance and sing. The boy agrees to give them away in exchange for her pulling up her dress, and so she does. Later on, the king announces that the princess will be wed to a man who can tell what symbols are on her body. Only the swineherd knows she has a moon on her thighs and stars on her breasts, and so they marry and live happily ever after. The man who gets the princess is the one who has seen her naked, who knows her body, and she is not punished for showing him. What a beautiful, refreshing 'moral of the story' in a sea of fairytales that teach us girls to be chaste and proper!

NWR: There is a lot that goes unsaid in between the lines and in the blank spaces of this book, giving readers room to reflect and come to their own conclusions. What conclusions do you suppose people will arrive at?

NH: Any form of art is essentially communication with its recipient, and any-one's perception of any work is going to be strongly influenced by their own unique set of experiences and opinions, so I believe it is impossible to guess this correctly. What I could describe instead is some sort of ideal reader, a person who I would like to speak to, with confidence that we will understand each other. This person would enjoy the flow of words and sentences, they would appreciate how the book is written and composed. They would want to read hungrily, intrigued, but not surprised by what they are reading; perhaps they are a woman or a girl, and they find certain situations familiar. They are aware that what happens in my book is not the unique case we all wish for it to be, but rather something terrifyingly common in our patriarchal society. Yet, they would still be disgusted – and rightly so. They would have to put the book down and take a break from it, and they would understand that my depicting this story as disgusting is purposeful and indicative of my opinion on the matter, even if I did not explicitly state my opinion in the text Occasionally, they would laugh, because I intended some parts to be funny, to help them let their guard down before the next punch in the gut. That is what I wish my readers would think and feel after reading my book, but I can only hope.

NWR: How do you feel about this book being translated into different languages? Have these translations captured the essence of the original text? Especially given that the work comes across as poetic and abstract, do you think a translation can have the same impact?

NH: From experience, I would even say it can make it better! After reading the Hungarian translation, for example, I concluded that I should have written the book in Hungarian from the start; that it is the language in which the words sound exactly how I wanted them to. I am also very excited about the English translation – I trust Julia Sherwood completely: that she understands my vision, and reading her translation absolutely confirmed it for me.

NWR: How do you feel about the upcoming adaptations of your work into film and theatre, considering the closeness of literary translation and adaptation into a different artform?

NH: To be completely honest, I am always very nervous about any adaptation. I am what you would call a control freak – after all, that is the reason I chose writing over other forms of art, because it gives me complete control over the final form of my work. There is minimal teamwork in being a writer, and I like it that way. So, regarding the theatre adaptations, I actually gave the directors complete creative freedom, otherwise they would start to absolutely despise me and regret they ever started working on my book at some point in the process.

Film is a completely different case, though, and I try to be as involved as possible. We even discussed a few scenes that did not make it into the book, because they would be painfully boring to read, but could be captivating in an audiovisual form. I am yet to read the script, and I try to be curious and optimistic.

NWR: How does your artistic background play out in your writing, particularly bearing in mind how abstract some of your descriptions are, challenging the reader's imagination to the extent that some may seem as surreal as a Dalí painting?

NH: I do not think it was an entirely conscious decision on my part, to write abstract descriptions and evoke surrealist paintings. I believe it's more connected simply to the way I think every day – my brain throws all these associations at me all the time, everything reminds me of something else, and then it eventually becomes this snowball of thoughts and images, and then, next to each other, they often change into something entirely new. Perhaps that could be called surrealist in essence, sure, but it all happens naturally, not as a part of some creative concept – I think the same way when I cook or talk to my partner about his day.

I also resist the word 'surreal' for a different reason, and that is because my goal was actually to write something very real, maybe even more true than everyday life, in a sense. During an average day, we usually do not have enough time to stop and think deeply about what we saw and how we feel about it, we do not talk to each other about our deepest fears and regrets when we meet in a café. Not because that would be shallow or ignorant, but maybe we do not like going that deep in public, where anyone could hear us, or we suddenly feel embarrassed, face to face with another human being who could judge or misunderstand us. Perhaps we are afraid we won't be able to find the right words to express ourselves. And that's completely fine. What art or literature gives us is a space to process all of that – we read a book alone, safely, with enough time on our hands to stop and think, without anyone impatiently waiting for our response. I write slowly, with enough time to choose my words. To circle back to surrealism: for me, it's not about using randomness to create something surprising or to evoke the absurd nature of a dream, rather, it's the other way around: it's meticulous sorting and making sense of life. For the reader to understand what I want to convey on an emotional level, I then sometimes use descriptions that may feel surreal, but are still very familiar. Take metaphors about the body, for example – I use them often, because we all have bodies and can therefore easily decipher the hidden meaning behind the metaphor. We all had a hair in our mouth at least once, so we understand it means 'gross', even when the author pushes that image to its limits.

For me, my artistic background [in graphic design and illustration] is most evident in the structure of the book. The short paragraphs were not inspired by poetry, but rather based on design principles, such as the use of white space. I also considered how a book works as an object: if I hide the 'punchline' on a completely different page, your eyes cannot skip the paragraphs in which I build the tension, you are forced to read them. You are also forced to turn the pages quite often, since there aren't many words printed on them, and subconsciously you are going to think: wow, what a page-turner! Those are the aspects of reading and writing that I enjoy exploring, and which arose directly from my education in arts and design.

NWR: Why did you choose to write a novella, to use words, as your art form for this piece? As an artist you could have illustrated this concept,

especially considering how visual the descriptions are; do you think that a novella is the most appropriate form for this story and why?

NH: It would be hilarious if I said no to this, wouldn't it? But I guess I did not think about it that way at all: I simply knew I wanted to write a good book, and to do that, this was the story I needed to focus on. In retrospect, there were undoubtedly other things that influenced my decision, like having a much bigger and more supportive community in the literary world than in the visual arts. I also had no idea how I would get any artwork to a bigger audience, but I did know what to do to get my text published. Currently, as I am working on what will hopefully be my second book, I thought about choosing the art form to express myself much more deliberately, as I had a concept for a series of paintings on the topic I also want to write about. Do you know what made me finally decide? The size of my flat. It would simply be madness to make and then store the paintings in the size I wanted them to be. So, I decided on a book, which can be done on a small refurbished laptop, in an open license text editor. Or maybe these are all excuses, and I am simply naturally more of a writer than a visual artist, who knows?

NWR: Given that this novella has become a controversial bestseller, as it were almost packaged as 'an uncomfortable and disturbing read', do you think that one of art's purposes is to unsettle our emotions in this way?

NH: I feel like I already touched on this a little bit in my previous answers without you even directly asking about it. So, very obviously, yes. We tend to think about art in such a cold manner – we analyse it, we try to be objective when reviewing it, we consume it too quickly, because there are just so many artworks to see and books to read! And we do this, of course, because we are taught to do so, to find the one right answer to why the curtains are blue; we are told we will not understand art without knowing history or the entire biography of the artist. And while those things are indeed important, they are by far not everything there is to art. It's interesting how music is the one exception – we do not feel the need to analyse the notes and know the historical background to be able to dance to Abba. I wish we would all learn to experience other forms of art as we do music. Ideally, we would let ourselves adore a painting simply because we are captivated by a particularly beautiful shade of colour, or connect to a character from a book only because they remind us of a childhood friend. We would find comfort even in artworks labelled 'disturbing', because it would assure us that at one point, someone else felt the same grief or anger we do. All kinds of art could provide us with a platform for feeling understood, and help us learn to understand others. It could be a space for us to feel less alone in this big world, and I find that more important now than ever.

Imogen Davies was educated in Wales and at Durham University but is currently based in Edinburgh, where she is completing post-graduate studies.

This Room Is Impossible to Eat *is out in hardback (£11) this spring from Parthian.*

WOLF COUNTRY

STORY BY **DOMINIKA MORAVČÍKOVÁ**
TRANSLATED FROM THE SLOVAK BY **ISABEL STAINSBY**

WE LIVE IN A BEAUTIFUL PART OF THE BORDER REGION.
The road isn't tarmacked; it's only an access road made of prefabricated concrete slabs. A gravel path or muddy track leads between the houses. Our hamlet doesn't have a name, any famous history, a coat-of-arms, a recognisable point on Google Maps, or even a website. Many people wouldn't believe that it's possible to live in such a godforsaken place in the modern era, but our hamlet is such a place, possibly even the last one. There's no post office here, or town hall, or church. We don't need any of them, because everything is close by, half an hour's walk to the nearest village, or fifteen minutes by car to town.

Our father taught us that being happy means knowing what needs to be done, when and with what tools. Digging after rain, burning hardwood in the smokery. Saying nothing you don't need to say, expecting nothing from no one. Doing what is required, and no more. That's the recipe for a good life. And we live well.

***

I have two brothers. Milan and Ondro. They're both foresters. They look after the forest and run a sawmill, the only business in our hamlet. Their hair is thick and spiky and their veins stand out on their faces. They're both unmarried. They probably always will be.

I was the first to be married, to the sawyer Števo. A quiet, decent, local lad. He doesn't drink or smoke. He rarely goes out in clothes other than his boiler suit with orange ear protectors and helmet.

A year after my wedding, my sister Iňa brought home an American. His name is Jathan but everyone calls him Jat. This made my parents think of džatky dumplings, a local speciality made with potatoes. That's why my mum cooked them for him the first time he pulled up in front of our house in his white Volvo. Iňa got out of the car and waded through the mud in her stilettos, while Jat bent down to look at the wheels. A sharp stone on the road had left him with a puncture.

'We'll repair it,' my father declared.

He brought out a roll of thick adhesive tape. Jat gesticulated wildly.

'Take him inside, Iňa,' our father ordered. 'Tell him to get the tyre changed on the main road, because he'll get another puncture on the way back. I'll pump it up, don't worry!'

Iňa ushered Jat into the house and our mum put a full plate on the table in front of him. She poured him a glass of milk and a shot of vodka while he chewed his dumplings.

Once it was dark, my father and both brothers joined him at the table. I kept on washing the glasses as they carried on chatting.

'Are you going to live in this house with us?' our father asked.

Jat didn't understand.

'Here, house, eat, drink, sleep, yes?'

Iňa blushed and took Jat's hand. 'We'll build our own house. We're buying the plot right next door. We've already called the old owner, you know who. It's all in hand.'

My father's mouth dropped open and he leant back in his chair, interested. 'Well, I never....'

Jat nodded constantly, and shook my father's hand after every translated sentence and every shot.

Midnight came and Iňa left the men and went to bed. I'd offered to take care of them.

Once my mum had gone to bed too, Jat and my father were getting on rather well. My father came up with the idea of extending the family land a little further, to the edge of the forest.

'That's just a scrap', was his opinion of the land that he was planning to buy with Iňa. 'We'll extend it by the plot a little way through the forest and connect it with our garden. So you can also have a woodshed, and a sauna, if you like, made of wood, of stone, even glass, whatever you want, yeah? I'll take care of it, that's the best way to do it.' My father fished the forestry catalogue out of the sideboard. 'Over here,' he said, opening the book and stabbing his finger at a picture. 'The plot, attached, space for a house.'

Jat thought of something and tapped words into the translation app on his phone. 'Per-miss-ion.'

He emphasised the word with the papers he took out of a leather bag.

'Haha,' said Father, sitting down and slapping him on the shoulder. 'No need, son.'

Jat was still rustling the papers. Father snatched them from him and shrugged demonstratively. 'Not needed, get it? You build here, at the edge of the forest, nobody sees, nobody hears. Not here, not like where you're from. Do you understand me? We're in the mountains here.'

'Mountains.'

'Exactly! Let's drink to it! Bottoms up!'

A few days later, Jat and Iňa came to visit again. As soon as they'd parked, they met some men in suits and signed a contract. Meanwhile, my father had started haggling with the neighbour about the forest covering some of the land, which was crossed not by the access track, but another one. He requested that this track be removed so the land could be used for other, private, purposes. He'd also started cooking up a timetable for building the house. While we were eating dinner, I told everyone that Števo and I were expecting our first child. It was an important announcement that briefly surpassed the urgency of my sister and Jat's concerns. My brothers dripped melted butter and wax onto my belly. Jat looked at me searchingly with a glass of cognac he'd brought from his homeland and laughed every now and then at Father's jokes. We saw he was beginning to understand whole sentences.

Then he and Iňa vanished for a month. When they reappeared, a lorry full of building materials was following Jat's car. My father was in his element. He walked along the forest track, his pipe in his mouth, and showed the lorry where to turn. My brothers and I ran up to the newly purchased land and helped to unload cement bags and roofing.

The men began to dig on the following day. Jat was glad that he'd abandoned the idea of a prefabricated wooden building with pre-made panels and informed Iňa that a stylish log cabin of spruce wood would be best. He'd employed an architect for the construction, and he arrived in the hamlet with his son and apprentice, who was carrying his briefcase, helmet and tools and mostly didn't dare open his mouth.

'Everyone wants something different today,' prattled the architect. "Outside, a cottage of crooked logs, like a painting of a fairytale village; inside, a casino with a jacuzzi.'

Iňa insisted that her land needed a high stone wall around it. 'Because of the wild animals.'

The architect was convinced that a stone wall wasn't appropriate for a cottage.

'Are you afraid of wolves?' I laughed.

'We have different wolves here, you know,' Iňa explained to the architect in a lowered voice. 'They're very bold. They'll come right onto your veranda.' She also added a comment about those wolves in our region who were born as human men, or so it was rumoured. The architect did not understand. He remarked that the area this close to the border was certainly swarming with smugglers and you *should* be afraid of them.

'Wolf packs inspect houses to find a place for their children,' Iňa went on, her tone conspiratorial.

The empathetic architect, doggedly insisting he respected local culture and folklore, approved the stone wall.

The building works dragged on throughout my entire pregnancy.

I first felt my contractions when I was pushing a wheelbarrow of bricks. My brothers and Jat plus the architect came running from the half-built wall.

'Put her in here.' Father pushed the wheelbarrow so close that it hit my ankles.

Jat began to unload the bricks and throw them onto the ground. The neighbour's mongrel, who often roamed around the building site and got under everyone's feet, was hit on the paw. The architect picked him up and threw him into the dug-out cellar. Meanwhile, my mother had put a towel under my behind, to take the chill off the flakes of fresh mortar on the bottom of the wheelbarrow. 'You're as pale as death,' she said to Jat, 'and this one isn't even yours, haha.'

'Well, I don't know,' grumbled the architect, who'd used his stylus to scrape mortar from the wheelbarrow corners, as if it mattered. 'You'd be better off calling an ambulance. Look at her!'

My father declared that we'd be able to drive to town more quickly than an ambulance could get out here.

'I'll drive,' Jat croaked, and ran to get his bag with the keys.

I was in labour for maybe ten hours. Števo arrived in his overalls and safety boots, ear protectors round his neck, on the evening bus. He sat down on an un-upholstered chair and took his son into his arms, all freshly bathed.

My father opened a bottle of plum brandy and poured out shots. He'd brought it from the pub below the hospital.

'Hopefully he won't be a wolf.'

'Let him not be a wolf,' my mum repeated as her toast.

Jat finished building the cottage a few days after the birth. He'd had satellite dishes installed, for picking up foreign television stations, and had extravagantly employed a company to do the final cleaning.

During the house-warming party, Father pulled me into the smoking room off the lounge. Iňa grandiosely called it the billiard room.

'We need to arrange a few trades.'

Trades was what my father called transfers of goods across the Polish border. He and my brothers undertook trades most often during the blueberry season.

I objected. 'What's that got to do with me?'

'We need three people to make it worthwhile. I can't traipse across the mountain any more, not on these legs.' He pulled up his trouser leg to display swelling caused by his diabetes. 'You'll go with your brothers.'

'Let Iňa go.'

Jat came into the side room. Father bowed to him and pointed at the wolfskin pinned to the wall. 'Where's that from?'

'I bought it,' Jat answered, in flawless Slovak.

'You'd be better off hiding it in the attic, mate.'

The following day, I took my son to the brook, water fresh from the mountains. The sun sparkled on the ripples and, when I jumped from stone to stone, holding him tight, I felt his breath, barely noticeable, like the movement of a fan, and his small heart beating with a delicate strength that was destined to become more powerful. I had to shade my eyes with my fingers to see my brother Milan, who was whistling at me from the opposite bank of the stream. He was pulling a cart full of cardboard boxes; shreds of tobacco, still burning, were falling from his roughly rolled cigarette. Once he'd finished whistling he disappeared inside with the cart, and Ondro half-closed the door. 'Give the little one to Mum on the veranda.'

By the time I'd got back from the veranda and arrived at the shed, my brothers were already unpacking the goods from the boxes. They counted the individual items and wrapped them in plastic sacks. Ondro prepared the bags for the blueberries.

Angrily, I kicked the old, stained bathtub that was kept in the shed, and it resounded like a bell.

'Calm down,' Ondro said. 'I don't get why you're still permanently snappy a month after the birth.'

'You wonder that she's worried about the baby?' Milan mused. 'The blueberries aren't growing that thickly. We're going to have to cover the goods up somehow.' He straddled a log and stamped out his cigarette.

'It'll work.'

***

Iňa and Jat were married in July. My brothers came up with a prank. An hour after midnight, they kidnapped the bride, as was the tradition, and sent Jat to look for her. Someone told him that it was a tradition and that Iňa would probably be in the roadside café by the main road, or somewhere near the stream. Jat walked to the café with an entourage of singing men. There our father delayed him by ordering champagne for the regulars and giving Jat some of his home-distilled elderberry brandy. Meanwhile, my brothers had summoned me to the stream and dressed me in Iňa's wedding dress.

'We have to have fun, even if Dad gets hanged,' Milan remarked, a crumpled cigarette between his teeth, as he laced my corset.

I was ready by the time Jat staggered up to me. I was sitting on the bench, tracing shapes on the water in my stockinged feet.

'Ingrid!'

I gave him my hand and he helped me to stand up. He tried to kiss me but I covered my face with the veil. He recognised me by my laugh and took a confused step back.

'Come with me.'

I took his hand and dragged him into the shed. When we entered, Milan, standing by the woodpile, was lighting an oil lamp. Ondro was leaning on the edge of the table, which was covered with tools.

'So here we are, then,' he began. 'You aren't stupid, you can get by and you know how to do business. In time you'll discover that this sawmill here doesn't earn shit.' He picked up the pliers and clicked them idly. 'Just so you know. We have our own ways here. And that's not going to change.'

Jat stood up straight and nodded.

Milan came up to him, grasped his ears and pressed his forehead to Jat's. 'Take care of our little sister.'

***

For many generations, we have had a family tradition of gathering blueberries. We don't use a berry picker comb, but pluck them lovingly, by hand. It takes longer, but we don't have to separate out the small twigs, and our berries are never squashed in the comb's teeth.

At the end of August, when the blueberries started to fruit properly, Iňa pulled on surgical gloves over her hands, gel nails and all, and she and Jat started joining our expeditions. Jat was fast and neat. Ondro confiscated every pail he filled, pouring the contents into a bag, so that plenty of blueberries could be scattered over dismantled weapons the following day. Then my brothers and I would make regular trips, traipsing across the mountains with a bag of blueberries on our backs until mid September, while Iňa took care of my child.

When all the trades were behind us and the season was over, my father decided that it was time to pierce little Janko's ear. It's an old custom in our hamlet. Boys have the upper part of the left earlobe pierced, then a silver earring with a bead is inserted.

"I don't like tagging children like that," Ingrid complained. "Are you a sheep now, too? Up the duff every year?"

Iňa was not happy about my second pregnancy. The reason wasn't clear to me. Maybe she was annoyed that I'd had a head start having children. And maybe she was afraid that our parents would now start to focus all their attention on my expanding branch of the family.

My second son was born in April. At the time, my brothers were in the tractor, ploughing Father's fields, and I was indicating where they should turn. Suddenly I felt my skirts get wet and I instantly flagged them down. Ondro turned off the engine, jumped from the tractor and carried me across the field. He pushed the fabric out of the way with his elbows, so my waters could fall to the ground.

He laid me on a mossy tuft at the edge of the stream and whistled to Milan. Then, between them, they lifted me and led me through the stream to the shed. They wanted to deliver my child there, so as not to soil the carpets in the house. After my first successful birth, they didn't consider it necessary to take me to hospital.

Ondro pulled out the stained bathtub from the corner and shredded tar soap into it. He hauled the garden hose from the other side of the stream, filled the bathtub with warm water directly from the boiler in the cellar and poured in a bottle of spirits, too. He stripped naked, slid into the water and scrubbed his own skin and some tools. Then he closed the door and got to work. He pulled off all my clothes and bent towards my ear. 'This will be over before you know it,' he assured me.

He cut the umbilical cord with the scissors he used for clipping hens' wings. He didn't hand me my son immediately, but took him out, still naked, into the fresh air, to 'show him our country', or so he said. On returning to the shed, he whispered something into the baby's ear. He didn't wash him but laid him, still bloody, on my chest.

A moment later Jat arrived with towels. 'Please God, let this child be human,' he declared, as he'd learned from us, and flung the towel over the new-born child spread out over my breasts and belly.

***

Six months after the log cabin was completed, Jat and my father were still building a stone wall around the plot of land at weekends. The neighbour's itinerant dog was still running around the site and, one moment when nobody was looking, he fell into a trough of concrete, where he drowned and set solid. My father discovered this by chance, when he dug a shovel into the mixture and hit the body.

He combed his hair, put on aftershave, took a bottle of home-distilled brandy and set out to see the neighbour. I went with him, taking the pram with the children too.

'Soooo,' said Father, sprawling on the bench on the veranda and clasping his hands, 'that shaggy dog of yours, what's his name again?'

The neighbour took fright. 'What have you done to him?'

'I didn't do anything. He jumped into my concrete off his own bat. Just when the girls had finally learnt to mix the cement properly! Up to now they've been making such thin shit. Murphy's law, I guess.'

The neighbour put his face into his hands and refused to talk to us any more. My father indicated to me that our visit was over and we left the veranda together. But then the neighbour thrust his head through the rails and bellowed: 'Your foreign sorcerer will only bring you bad luck, I tell you! Look what he's turned your daughter Iňa into! She's as stingy as the day is long!'

My father went red. 'What?!'

'I'm right, aren't I?' screeched the neighbour. 'She's managing her husband's property. And what about your sons? Where are their brides? They crawl around the brothels and on Saturday night one of them pissed in my garden! And that's not the only thing that's wrong with them! They're not right! As if we didn't all know what those two really are!'

'I'm warning you,' said my father, raising a finger. 'You keep your filthy trap shut!'

The neighbour snorted and went into his house.

My father grabbed the pram and forced its wheels through the damp soil as if it were a plough.

***

I started to take my older son with me on trades with blueberries. On the last one, he turned red and got a fever. This had never happened before. I squealed and hit my brothers on the chest. 'He's burning up, we have to find help!'

The customs house was closer than our hamlet and we couldn't reach my father on the phone.

'Screw you, I'm going to the customs house. Maybe they'll have some medicine there, and we can call an ambulance.'

'Little sister... we can't do that.'

'Just try and stop me. Or I'll go and report you all.'

'Fine, just chill, okay?' said Ondro, breathing deeply and clearly starting to think intensely.

Milan sat down under a tree and lit up.

'We'll bury them.'

We poured the blueberries out of the bags. We threw the weapons into a hole, then tore up some small shrubs to cover it. Finally we refilled the bags with blueberries and headed north.

At the customs house, they examined my son and gave him some medicine from their first-aid kit to bring down his temperature. We stacked the blueberry bags in a corner of the office. One police officer wanted to see what we'd gathered.

Milan raised his hand. 'Be my guest.'

'We don't use a berry picker comb,' I said.

The customs officer tasted two blueberries. 'Yuck, they're sour! Where did you pick them?'

'I don't know what you call these mountains,' Milan grumbled.

Within an hour the medicine started to work. My child settled, cooled down and fell asleep.

'Let's get out of here,' Milan whispered to me.

'It's dark,' I objected.

'We'll sleep in the mountains.'

My brothers stood up and put on their anoraks.

***

'Pssst....'

Ondro woke me up by pulling on my ear, as he always used to when we were kids.

The fire had almost gone out. I instantly knew that they were near us. Maybe it was the smell or the barely perceptible sounds of paws on the rotting leaves.

'What is it?' I whispered.

He squeezed my hand. 'Take a good look.'

In the gloom I made out wolf silhouettes.

'They've surrounded us,' he said. 'No sudden movements. Wake Milan.'

Milan was lying on my other side. I snuggled up to his head and covered him with my body, so he didn't twitch as he woke up.

'Don't look around,' Ondro motioned. 'Lie on your backs and count the stars.'

I gazed at the familiar constellations. My neck felt warm from my child's breath, which was weak but regular. I broke out into a sweat every time the leaves rustled under the wolves' paws. I was expecting animal saliva to drip onto my face at any moment, or to see their eyes flashing.

'Iveta, we should try to sleep. They'll go away.'

'They're still too close.'

'You're just imagining that.'

'Sleep.'

***

I dreamt that I woke up. Instead of my brothers, two wolves were lying beside me. In my dream I was expecting this. As if they'd been like that before too, but just hadn't looked like it.

Some men are wolfish. I'd been taught that since I was very small. 'As if we didn't all know what those two really are,' the neighbour had said. They're nothing like our parents. I should have noticed that long ago. They're nothing like any of us.

Maybe the pack had ordered us to spend a night in the forest. Maybe they wanted to take them back. Or merely to see them again. To inspect them. To judge their souls.

'They've gone,' Ondro pronounced, once I was really awake.

Sharp rays slanted across his face. I thought he looked younger.

***

My third child was to be born in the summer. We no longer saw Jat very often. Mostly he holed up in the house or festered in the pub with the regulars. There were periods when he neither washed nor shaved, but traipsed from the houses to the edge of the forest and back again, wearing the old overalls in which he'd slaved over the building, years ago.

Iňa had inherited from our father a sort of art of dealing with tricky business. She took it into her head to have a ramp built on the path to the log cabin. She obtained planning permission, a ramp and a notice reading 'Private property'.

My brothers thought that Jat was behind this. At night they climbed onto the roof and cut the internet and TV cables.

When they learned that it was actually Iňa's work, they cornered her at the food store and escorted her to the shed, where I was waiting for the three of them with a kerosene lamp. Ondro grabbed his pliers and began to click them idly.

'So, what's up with you, then, huh?'

Iňa flicked a strand of hair behind her shoulder, like she always did. 'What do you want? Money? We aren't like you. Or like the others in the hamlet.'

'But you will be,' Ondro laughed. 'It's high time!'

***

Jat got his ear pierced with a bead. He came to my brothers of his own voli-tion. Mum gave him her grandfather's earring. I pierced his ear myself with a nail gun, on the sofa in his house, while Iňa was in town.

When Iňa returned home and saw us, she looked as if she'd caught Jat cheating on her. Her husband explained the ritual value of the new earring, but even so, Iňa considered it a betrayal. She led me into the billiard room and told me that being permanently pregnant had caused me to lose my common sense. 'You're jealous of me, aren't you? You married the boy next door and even so it's Milan and Ondro that take care of you. I hope you realise that they aren't even our brothers.'

'You're so stupid,' I said. 'At least I'm safe with them.'

'Because you're bringing up wolf children,' she replied scornfully. 'I won't let the same thing happen to mine.'

Then I told her of my suspicion that something was wrong, as she hadn't fallen pregnant. Iňa snapped that everything was fine, both psychologically and gynaecologically, the doctor was permanently monitoring her and she'd only come off the pill recently, because she'd wanted to wait until their accommodation was sorted.

'But everything is done now,' she sighed.

She gradually began to completely avoid our brothers, and a few months later she and Jat quietly moved into town, back into a rented flat. All the signs showed that this was better for Jat. He returned to the company of his anglophone city boys and rapidly forgot the mores and rituals of our region. It was practically impossible to sell the cottage, but finally it was purchased by a wealthy family who only showed up at weekends.

Iňa and Jat went to live in the south, far away from our hamlet and the high mountains.

I met up with her again only when she'd had a child. Unfortunately for her, it was a boy, but she did everything possible to ensure he had nothing to do with wolves. She played the piano for him, dressed him in pure wool, rubbed rare oils into his skin. She was convinced that she'd avoided fate and not become a surrogate for wolf children. She admitted to me that she still had bad dreams about our hamlet, our brothers and the wolf pack that lurked in the woods.

'If we don't stop it, they'll keep on multiplying, along the male line, never in the female. And in the end, the world will only have wolf men,' she prophesied in a whisper, as if the child resting his little head on her chest could understand her words and be scared.

***

We live in a beautiful part of the border region.

We dig after rain, we burn hardwood in the smokery. We have everything we need from our own work. We don't say much; nothing we don't need to say.

My sons are already pretty independent. I give them plenty of toys, but they always want to play with each other, not with things. They compete in the mud and the sandpit, they fight naked in the bathroom, they stab each other with their fingers in different parts of their bodies. Most of all they love to play on my belly. They have scratched and bitten me many times now.

In the evenings I put them to bed. I forbid them from running around and talking, even though I know that they will dart out from under their quilts as soon as I've closed the door.

In the morning, when the fire has gone out, they'll play in the hearth, drawing pictures with their fingers in the ash and then, giggling, they'll tear firelighter boxes to shreds.

Before the sun comes up.

Translator's acknowledgements: my thanks to Conor Daly, Gwen Davies, Dominika Moravčíková, Monika Polakovičová, David Pritchard and Julia Sherwood.

Dominika Moravčíková is a fiction writer and poet based in Košice, Slovakia. One of the most exciting young voices in contemporary Slovak literature, she debuted in 2020 with the poetry collection *Deti Hamelnu* (*The Children of Hamelin*). The book received widespread critical acclaim across Slovakia and Czechia. In 2022, she published her second book, a collection of short stories entitled *Dom pre Jeleňa* (*The Deer House*). The stories, characterised by Moravčíková's imaginative use of language and world-building through the development of fictional rural mythologies, have also received much attention since they were published. In 2019, she became the first writer to win both the country's short story prize, Poviedka, and the poetry prize Básne SK–CZ in the same year. Her works have been translated into five languages. 'Wolf Country' is from Dominika's collection *The Deer House*.

Isabel Stainsby has been working in the translation industry since 2010. She has a BA in German and Czech with Slovak, an MA in Slavonic Studies, and the Diploma in Translation in both French to English and German to English. She is a member of both the Chartered Institute of Linguists and the Institute of Translation and Interpreting. Isabel has a number of literary translations under her belt, ranging from science fiction novels to academic books and articles. Recent publications include *The True Way Out*, a memoir by Czech Roma journalist Patrik Banga, published by CEEOL Press; 'The Cat', a short story by Czech author Petra Soukupová and 'People and Nations, Cross Borders!', an essay by Slovak writer and journalist Márius Kopcsay, both in the *Continental Literary Magazine*. Her translation of Slovak writer Barbora Hrínová's *Unicorns*, a short story collection, will be published by Seagull Books in 2026. She is currently working on another science fiction novel, by Czech author Jan Kotouč, and a novella by Slovak author Jana Bodnárová. She lives in Glasgow.

THE MAKING – AND UNMANNING – OF THE WELSH COLLIER

CHRIS MOSS DISCOVERS A RICH SEAM OF REFLECTIONS IN A COMPARATIVE HISTORY, A REPACKAGED WORK OF NONFICTION AND AN ESSAY COLLECTION

Books Under Review
The Shadow of the Mine: Coal and the End of Industrial Britain, Huw Beynon and Ray Hudson (Verso, 2021)
Miner's Day, BL Coombes and Isabel Alexander, ed Peter Wakelin (Parthian, 2021)
Representing the Male: Masculinity, Genre and Social Context in Six South Wales Novels, John Perrott Jenkins (UWP, 2021)

COAL MINERS HAVE ALWAYS BEEN DEALT THE WORST HAND. IN THE early days, when they clustered in hovels near pitheads, they were regarded as outcasts and oddballs, denizens of the dark. When their industry was booming, their workplace remained horrendously primitive, often lethal, and their wages insultingly low. When they sided with a political party – Labour – it repeatedly betrayed them. When they created a national union for a nationalised industry, the NUM and NCB at times colluded and acted chiefly in their own institutional political interest. When the technology finally improved, the market collapsed.

When they went on strike against the Thatcher government, which had declared war on them and their communities, they stood largely alone – facing police forces intent on breaking their own rules about protecting the public. Ex-miners, resident in the poorest towns, were considered unskilled and unemployable. Many suffered from pneumoconiosis and silicosis, for which life-shattering conditions they were granted derisory compensation.

From the mid 1980s, coal mining has been disappeared from British history. Headgear was torn down, shafts capped, slagheaps flattened and landscaped. Then came one final slur: when the world realised coal had helped heat the planet up to a dangerous level, coal miners could not but be seen as part of the problem. The black faces of the past were like the skies over forests, and our probable future.

Yet, they were heroes. Yet, they were legends. Yet, everybody liked and admired and trusted miners, in some obscure way. Miners' children inherit a strange, complicated pride and some shame, for no other job is as real and useful as was mining for heat and light underground. (A disclosure: my father was a coal miner.)

I must use the past tense; for miners are as prone to untimely deaths as World War One soldiers, and their number is fast diminishing.

There is already a substantial library of books about coal mining and its decline. *The Shadow of the Mine: Coal and the End of Industrial Britain* by Huw Beynon of Cardiff University and Ray Hudson of the University of Durham, is a valuable and interesting addition. Its retelling of the story comprises a brisk account of the rise of the industry and a more detailed history of its apogee and implosion; the most novel element is that the narrative splices together the coalfields of south Wales and County Durham.

While the two areas had similarly challenging coalfaces, thanks to their respective geologies, they had very different histories. Mining began in County Durham in the sixteenth century and grew steadily, reaching its high point in the early twentieth. South Wales mining only took off in the early nineteenth century, and the industry boomed extraordinarily from the 1880s. The regions also had divergent political and syndicalist histories, with south Wales a hard left, sometimes revolutionary, setting and Durham generally more moderate – at least until the end days when reaction radical-ised the ever-shrinking hardcore of mine workers.

What is striking about coal is how short-lived the boom period was: the heyday was half a century long, from 1880 to the Great Depression. But the sector employed more than a million men in the first decades of the twenti-eth century and more than 287 million tons of coal were extracted in a year. Coal powered the trains, mills and factories of the Industrial Revolution; as Orwell wrote, 'Our civilisation, *pace* Chesterton, is founded on coal.'*

By 1911, two thirds of the Welsh population were concentrated in the mining counties of Glamorgan and Monmouthshire; a decade later, the census recorded that a third of Wales' entire male labour force worked in the mines and quarries. These demographic convulsions shaped Welsh culture as violently as the borers and cutters changed the landscape of the Valleys.

Beynon and Hudson offer a very readable, fair-minded account of the evolution and erasure of the Welsh and Durham coalfields, liberally pep-pered with statistics and set against the broader history of industrialisation and wartime. They know about engineering as well as the social and political aspects of the industry, which helps explain how some coalfields prospered as technologies improved. Yorkshire and the Midlands were, they suggest, generally regarded as 'central' coalfields while Wales and, especially, County Durham, were for long periods marginalised.

What emerges, even before the apocalyptic mid Eighties, is a tale of caprice and abuse. Before unionisation, miners, to their lordly employers, were as expendable as tools or the rock itself. They were only needed when other industries needed the fuel, and were hired and fired, paid and under-paid, according to the whims of global trade.

Treated thus, communities in south Wales responded by establishing their own care networks in the form of chapels, welfare halls and librar-ies. This gave rise to a genuine working-class culture which provided the seedbed for the rise of socialism and of its diluted, Establishment form – the Labour Party. The miners' institutes of south Wales have been described by one historian as 'the greatest network of cultural institutions created by working people anywhere in the world'. The authors provide a lot of detail on how organisations such as the Durham Miners' Association – established in 1869 – and the Miners' Federation of Great Britain, founded following a gathering of local trade unions in Newport in 1888, sought to provide a platform for miners' grievances and demands.

The Depression was followed by the collapse of the second minority Labour government. In the aftermath of the 1931 election, unemployment hammered both Durham and south Wales. Pilgrim Trust researchers visiting Crook in 1936 found 71 per cent of unemployed miners had been out of work for more than five years. Over a tenth of miners were unemployed, while new industries such as car manufacture were far less impacted. A serious consequence of this was that the government focused on welfare and unemployment provision and treated mining as a regional rather than national problem. As the authors put it, 'Once identified with hard work and industry, they and their people were now treated as pathological.' Cruelly, places like south Wales had never been allowed to diversify their industries because of the risk of tempting miners out of the collieries.

This disregard for the ordinary miner's worth would characterise the Westminster view of coal in coming decades. When oil began to replace coal, and manufacturing was offshored, coal mining was viewed as an inconvenient Victorian legacy. This fall – in prestige, in economic importance – is the story that dominates the pages of *The Shadow of the Mine*. While there is no doubt that significant benefits were gained by the creation of the National Union of Mineworkers in 1945 and of the National Coal Board the following year, the symbiotic intimacy enjoyed by these two organisations often led to workers' needs being overlooked. The über-male environment of the pit also rubbed off on the suits and ties. One deputy manager is quoted as saying senior bosses, vying to be the next chairman, 'wanted to be the biggest macho-man in the coalfields'.

The denouement of the Seventies and Eighties, when mining towns were allowed to collapse, and miners made redundant without alternative work being made available, is one of the sorriest stories in British labour history.

Hateful characters like the bullying NCB boss Ian MacGregor and toadying Thatcherites like Nicholas Ridley stain many pages. The Downing Street Policy Unit was staffed by the heads of BP, Shell and the nuclear energy sector. During the Eighties, south Wales miners fared worst when it came to finding new jobs, with more than half of them unemployed by the end of the period. Those who moved on took up dead-end jobs at places like Unilever's Pot Noodle factory near Crumlin. At no stage in the winding-up of mining were coal miners and their families properly consulted, by their managers, by the government or, even, by their union; promises and lies emanated from all sides, giving the workers hope they might be spared. But the axe continued to fall, until the entire industry was destroyed.

What was lost? Ask many residents of south Wales or Durham today, and they might well reply 'Everything' – and be justified in that response. The relationship between coal and the two regions was forged in blood and fire, in disease and death. It's no wonder their descendants feel betrayed. As Beynon and Hudson, writing about the period 1981–89, eloquently put it:

> In the space of eight years, both Areas [sic] had experienced social trauma as families dealt with mine closures while still digesting the full consequences of the strike and how it had ended. The women who so solidly and bravely supported the strike would, at other times, have told you that they didn't want their sons to go underground; that they hoped that there would be 'something better' for them. But, failing that, 'there's always the pit'. In this and in other ways, the pit – and the jobs it provided – had been understood as the collective property of many mining villages: it was 'our pit'. These places, these holes in the ground, had become part of villagers' lives in detailed, deep and complex ways that were ruptured both during the strike and in its aftermath.

Anyone who wants to understand the desolation of south Wales' mining towns and villages, who wants to know about one of the central causes of the economic hardship of the nation, who wants to grasp why the job prospects for many people today are limited to solitary lorry driver, lorry-loader or 'logistics' warehouse drudge, should read this excellent work of social and industrial history.

To twenty-first century readers, BL Coombes' *Miner's Day* is a nostalgia trip and an extended epitaph. As he wrote in 1947, 'There is still a very deep pit between the mass of workers in this country and its intellectuals.' Twenty-five years after the supposed birth of Modernism, the latter group were still concentrated in London and in their Home Counties piles. Orwell's nonfiction writings were basically gritty travelogues, the well-meaning meanderings of an Etonian out of his element. Landmark novels like Walter Greenwood's *Love on the Dole* (1933) and Lewis Jones' *Cwmardy* (1937) had slightly dented the preconceived notions about class held by the literati, but they inevitably framed workers' experience within a web of emotional plotting and translated local colour.

Coombes felt it his duty to reset the relationship, and his bestselling autobiography *These Poor Hands* (1939), his more technically minded follow-up, *Those Clouded Hills* (1944), and the nonfiction *Miners Day*, first published as a slim paperback by Penguin books in 1945, was part of this ongoing project.

Coombes was born in 1893 in Wolverhampton but raised in south Wales, where his father was a miner at Treharris. The family moved to the Welsh/English borders between Hereford and Hay on Wye, to take on the tenancy of a small farm. But Coombes hated rural poverty and, when he was seventeen, moved to the Upper Neath valley – where he would stay for more than 40 years. The Empire colliery, where the mining was of the drift variety, and the nearby communities of Cwmgwrach and Blaengwrach, are the chief settings of his writings; *Miner's Day* – originally titled, oddly, *Miners Day* – is a first-person, present-tense narrative that seeks to capture the voice and movements of a group of miners. It's not a memoir nor is it a 'day in the life', as the events recounted range over several days, including Sunday, allowing the author to touch on arriving and leaving work, toil at the coalface and above ground, farming and Neath market, chapel and the choir, Bevin Boys and hard-grafting wives, accidents and a meeting to discuss striking. The most evocative sections are when Coombes shifts his gaze from the merely descriptive and the rigours of manual labour, and employs his considerable gifts to show something of the strangeness of the miner's existence.

On arriving at the pithead: 'My mates were coming from all directions, like an army of invaders who had surrounded their objective, towards that hole in the ground.'

On miners' self-absorption: '"Another blinkin' miner's weekend" was the emphatic grouse from some of the men on a Saturday morning... as if they considered this dampness would be a concern of their[s] alone; that it would not hinder the pleasure of anyone else.'

On weekends: 'During the weekend our mole-like existence fades from close consciousness, but is revived when we start again in that pit life which is our second nature.... That is the queerest part of it all – how swiftly we forget the problems of the pit; possibly because they are so far hidden from daylight.'

On chapel singing: 'Nearly always there is a drag about that sort of singing; the organ is just half a beat in front of the most confident voices and the others tail behind like the lame in a procession.'

Isabel Alexander, a Slade-trained artist, made three visits to the Valleys, including a rushed trip around Cwmgwrach with Coombes as guide [her black-and-white portraits of the Rhondda community are featured in these pages]. Her drawings and watercolours, which exhibit sympathies with Post-Impressionism and angular Vorticism as well as German New Objectivity, capture the desolation of the landscapes and in people's faces. Her grey palette emphasises a world bereft of natural light, as if the darkness of the mine seeps upwards and into the hills, streets and sky. Her renderings of twisted old rails and wire fences show how industrialisation was never about care, for people or for places; the seeds of post-industrial decline were already there in the Thirties. Given an opportunity to go underground to one of the levels at Blaencwm, part of the Glenrhondda Colliery, Alexander depicted a miner stooping. But there is no sense of a man – he is a large bear-like shadow, seemingly connected to the rock, silhouetted against the reflection of his lamp. Terraced houses look anonymous, and have a hard geometrical edge that disrupts the curve of hill and lane. Only the close-ups of miners' faces offer a glimpse into the dignity and weariness of the Welsh collier.

Taken together, Coombes' text and Alexander's illustrations make for an intriguing dialogue: the miner writing outwards, the artist drawing herself into the 'other' reality. The latter's images will have been as good as lost in the old cheaply made Penguin edition, and it is commendable that Parthian have rescued this important artistic duologue from a world that was always part-hidden and is now fully lost. The 'miner's day' ends with lungs shot by dust; death was always close at hand for these workers. Coombes, as a writer, had to remove himself from the daily grind to reflect on it, but he also hints that all miners have something of the loner about them, something of the alienated.

John Perrott Jenkins' *Representing the Male* will be of interest to a narrow niche of readers. For one thing, a satisfying reading will only be available for those who have read the six novels with which it is concerned: Gwyn Jones' *Times Like These* (1936); the aforementioned *Cwmardy*; Menna Gallie's *Strike for a Kingdom* (1937); *So Long, Hector Bebb* (1970), by Ron Berry; and two contemporary novels, Roger Granelli's *Dark Edge* (1997) and Kit Habianic's *Until Our Blood is Dry* (2014).

Masculinity is a 'contested' site. Once thought as solid as a wall of coal or, at least, a hewer's thigh, it is, in 2025, a hotly debated, derided, even ridiculed noun. In a public discourse that is increasingly gender-fluid, where being camp may be seen to be not only 'normal' but enlightened, being 'masculine' is at best meaningless and at worse, slightly silly, like being 'manly' used to be and being 'macho' was before that.

In his introduction, Jenkins outlines his argument, grounding it on the particularly Welsh stereotype of a chapel-singing, rugby-loving coal miner who is regarded by his community (or at least his pals) as something of a hero (or 'ledge', as Nessa Jenkins might put it). While this might seem significant progress from the aforementioned early-industrial era notion of the marginalised, mole-like miner, this author is not so sure:

> The image of the 'heroic' miner served the material demands of patriarchal industrial capitalism and gave the miner in return the small compensation of status, but the image of a transcendent masculinity, generated and promoted by this cultural system, was as unrepresentative of the individual self as it was of the mythic homogenised group.

He goes on to say this reductive image gave women secondary roles, while also hemming in the men. He then elaborates, by means of examples and close reading, how the six novels of varying quality subvert said ideal by showing complex individuals rather than ciphers. Which is, let's face it, what novels always do.

Jenkins' book, while worthy, reminded me why I never want(ed) to do a PhD. Though only 200 pages long, it felt like a lot more, as it is couched in turgid academese, with every tentative half-assertion and slender idea supported by some earlier reference – from the novels, but also from the works of Gramsci, Marx, Lacan, the usual suspects.

The problem here, I think, for me anyway, is that reading a critique of novels about miners is, inevitably, three steps removed from the miner himself. While everybody now feels obliged to reframe maleness in a new gender-skewing, essentialism-querying (and queering) dialectic, in the end it feels too late for that. There are no coal miners. The roles they played are gone. For sure, the memory of the male–female dichotomy matters, but so does the fact that all our mining fathers and grandfathers died too young – while their 'repressed' and socially constrained wives got an additional decade or more.

I find the verbatim answer of a pit deputy, when questioned about a lost sense of worth due to deindustrialisation, quoted in *The Shadow of the Mine*, more insightful than anything Jenkins has to say about his chosen novels:

The point you said about self-esteem, self-confidence and everything else is perfectly correct, but added to that, the grief of them losing the pits and everything is one thing, but the fact that women have taken over is also another thing, because we were the breadwinners, now we're the bloody housewives, so we resent the fact of women taking over. They may be the activists, but we don't want them to be, it's just that we have been so down in the dumps now that we don't give a monkey's who takes over, we're going into another system now, but the men don't count for naught.

Note
The Road to Wigan Pier (1937); Chesterton had written that civilisation 'is founded upon abstractions' (*Tremendous Trifles*, 1909).

Chris Moss is a travel writer and critic who is currently writing a book on 'untouristed' places, as showcased in his *Guardian* column (and previewed in his piece on Wrexham in these pages). He lives in the north-west of England.

[1] 'Young Miner, Rhondda', c1943, conté, 30 x 22cm. Isabel appears to have drawn this young miner after he came back from a shift, before he went into the baths. He is still black with coal dust and wearing his compressed-paper helmet and working clothes of scarf and jacket. The dust has caught in his stubble, but his lips and eyes are rubbed clean. (Collection: Glynn Vivian Art Gallery).

[2] 'WM [Winston Morgan], a Young Miner, Rhondda', 1943, conté, 37 x 27cm. Isabel recorded this young miner with the initial WM. BL Coombes wrote about his youthful colleagues with foreboding, knowing how quickly injury or pneumoconiosis could take away their futures. (Collection: Glynn Vivian Art Gallery).

ISABEL ALEXANDER: RHONDDA MINING PORTRAITS FROM THE 1940S

With thanks to Robin Alexander, Peter Wakelin, Bridgeman Images, the Glynn Vivian Art Gallery and the publishers for permission to reproduce images and text from Miner's Day *(Parthian 2021, £20) and* Rhondda Portraits *(Grey Mare Press 2024, £7). All images © estate of Isabel Alexander.*

BL COOMBES' *MINER'S DAY* WAS FIRST PUBLISHED AS A PENGUIN Special in 1945 with illustrations by Isabel Alexander. Parthian's sumptuous 2021 re-issue of this classic includes a much larger selection of the artist's Rhondda images and an essay by the book's editor, Peter Wakelin. He observes:

> It is hard to think of any other painter or photographer who made so many portraits of coal-mining families in the period: the elderly, young miners, mothers and children, all treated as individuals. [Isabel Alexander] was not trapped by the conventional portrayal of colliers black from the pit but looked instead at the men underneath the mask of dust, those who had retired through injury, and the women who kept families alive in desperate times.[1]

Finally realising a project conceived in 1944 but shelved, *Rhondda Portraits* combines the artist's Rhondda images with commentary by her husband Donald Alexander (who himself worked extensively in south Wales and was rated by the British Film Institute as 'arguably the key figure in the story of coal on film').[2] Editor Robin Alexander picks up Peter Wakelin's theme:

The intensity of Isabel's concentration on individual faces and circumstances perhaps compensates for what, as Dai Smith justly notes, is often missing from Rhondda portrayals by 'outsider' artists:

> The pulse of people living, out in the open, together... jostling each other on pavements, darting across carless roads before the packed, people-carrying double-deckers, or trotting imperiously down on horseback from the mountains, or leaning at an angle on each other to wend their way home after Sunday drinking in a workingmen's club.[3]

There are of course some rapidly sketched glimpses: women scrubbing their doorsteps or returning home with bags of shopping, children sliding down tips, men bearing sacks of discarded coal, a lone miner on his allotment; a woman carrying her baby in her shawl; but never the generously peopled streets of, say, Rhondda-born Charles Burton,[4] and most in any case positioned more to give scale and perspective to their surroundings than as the chief object of the artist's attention. This could be for the prosaic reason that drawing and painting were mostly done during the day, when the men were underground, the women engaged in indoor chores, and the children at school. But given that Isabel also went underground, and that she was free to draw at any time of day or night, it is possible – though we shall never know for certain – that what Peter Wakelin detects as a distinctive and positive focus in her work, and Dai Smith as a deficit in the work of her non-Welsh contemporaries, represented Isabel's conscious choice not to replicate what others were doing so well. Instead, she offers her own unique perspective on Rhondda through her portraits of men, women and children as individuals rather than as anonymous members of a crowd, and through the drama and abstraction of the forms she conjures from those mostly deserted streets, pitscapes and mountainsides.[5]

Endnotes

1 *Miner's Day*, BL Coombes and Isabel Alexander, ed Peter Wakelin (Parthian, 2021, p 37).

2 https://www.bfi.org.uk/features/if-you-enjoyed-when-coal-was-king

3 *Off the Track: Traces of Memory*, Dai Smith (Parthian, 2023, pp 38 and 267).

4 *Charles Burton*, Peter Wakelin (Sansom, 2019).

5 *Rhondda Portraits*, Isabel Alexander and Donald Alexander, ed Robin Alexander, (Grey Mare Press, 2024, pp 10–11).

6 *Isabel Alexander: Artist and Illustrator*, Janet McKenzie (Parthian, 2017)

The preceding and following illustrations by Isabel Alexander use Peter Wakelin's captions from the 2021 edition of *Miner's Day*. Some have been amended in light of information that emerged during the preparation of *Rhondda Portraits*.

Isabel Alexander (1910–1996) trained at Birmingham and the Slade. She produced socially engaged documentation of the lives of working people, vibrant landscapes and seascapes, abstracts and prints. Her Rhondda paintings, drawings and lithographs arose from extended working visits during 1943–45 when she was based in Tylorstown. Later she lectured in art education and during her lifetime had thirty-six joint and solo exhibitions. Fresh interest in this artist's life and work was prompted by the Mercer gallery's retrospective show and Janet McKenzie's in-depth study, *Isabel Alexander: Artist and Illustrator*,[6] both in 2017. Next came *Miner's Day* (2021) and *Rhondda Portraits* (2024), the two books extracted here. Meanwhile, some of her Rhondda portraits featured in the Glynn Vivian Gallery's 2022 exhibition *Art and Industry: Stories from South Wales*.

[3] 'EL[yle], the Overman, Blaencwm', 1943, lithograph, 39 x 32cm. The caption to this portrait in 'Coal: The National Plague Spot', 1946, said: 'EL is an overman – a sort of foreman or manager's deputy. He started work at eleven and has been at it for fifty-three years. His group gets the worst of both worlds – the men tend to think of it as on the owners' side, yet the wages are little above a collier's. EL, however, is well-liked – the men find him firm but fair.' Isabel noted that he worked at Blaencwm but she based the background on her drawings at Gilfach Goch.

[4] Tom Evans [TE], 1944, lithograph, 37 x 27cm. On a sketch for this lithograph, which appeared in the original edition of Miner's Day (1945), Isabel wrote: 'This man was suffering from nystagmus, a condition showing rapid to and fro movements in the eyeballs. With miners it is brought on by working for a long time underground in a poor light.'

[5] 'WI, Totally Disabled by Silicosis', c1943, pencil, 35 x 28cm. Dust disease is a repeated theme in the text of Miner's Day, and Isabel met several miners with pneumoconiosis whose portraits she drew. The disease itself could not be depicted, but her portraits capture the loss, indignity and tragedy that were its legacy. (Collection: Glynn Vivian Art Gallery).

[6] 'FM [Frank Morton], a Disabled Miner', 1943, pencil, 28 x 19 cm. This naturalistic portrait was the frontispiece to the 1946 essay 'Coal: The National Plague Spot'. It echoes Coombes' observations that men aged more quickly in the mines. 'FM' could be in his fifties but his face is drawn, his forehead marked by worry lines, and he stares into the uncertain future of a disabled worker. Isabel noted that she drew him in his greenhouse.

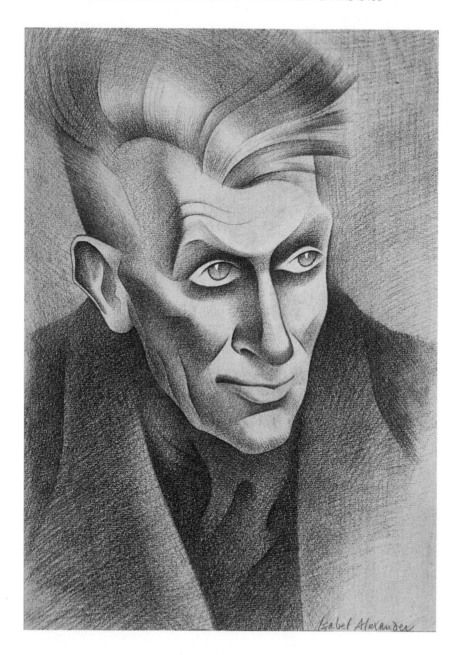

[7] 'Dan', 1944, lithograph, 34 x 24cm. Isabel wrote on this lithograph, made for publication in the original edition of Miners Day: 'LE, Totally Disabled from Silicosis' and on a photograph of it, that she had drawn him in his own home. In the book it was titled 'Dan' and accompanied the writer BL Coombes' tender description of his friend who was dying from dust disease. It seems likely that Isabel met him on her visit to the Neath valley. The original Conté drawing is in the Glynn Vivian Art Gallery.

[8] 'Mrs G[riffiths]', 1943, lithograph, 38 x 30cm. This extraordinary portrait parallels BL Coombes' comments about the lives of women in mining communities and the special economic challenges for families outside work. The lithograph was published in the illustrated essay 'Coal: The National Plague Spot' in 1946. The caption stated: 'Mrs G's husband is an ex-miner. Her sons and eldest grandson work in the pits. 53 shillings comes into her house every week. Rent is 12s 6d. Coal costs them 33s per ton, delivered. If Mr G were still at work he would pay 6s a ton at the pithead plus cartage.' The setting is Blaencwm: Isabel recalled she sketched Mrs G near her home.

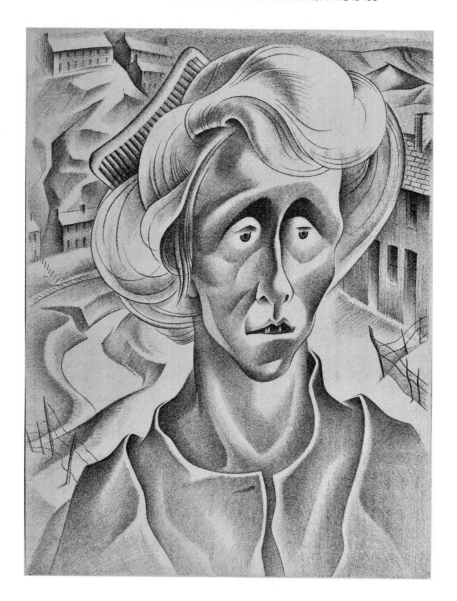

[9] 'Mrs C, Mother of Seven', 1943, lithograph, 41 x 31cm. Isabel noted that Mrs C was the mother of three of the children she drew and that the setting was near her home. It is a troubling portrait that goes beyond Isabel's habitual objectivity. In an otherwise warm review of an exhibition of Isabel's in The Studio, *January 1952, WJ Strachan picked out its 'almost brutal stylisation'. However, the distress was real of mothers who had starved themselves to feed their children through the Depression. Seven children would have meant a battle for survival, and Isabel noted that Mrs C's husband was among the long-term unemployed. Her up-to-date [for the time] hairstyle cannot diminish her gaunt frame, lost teeth and traumatised expression.*

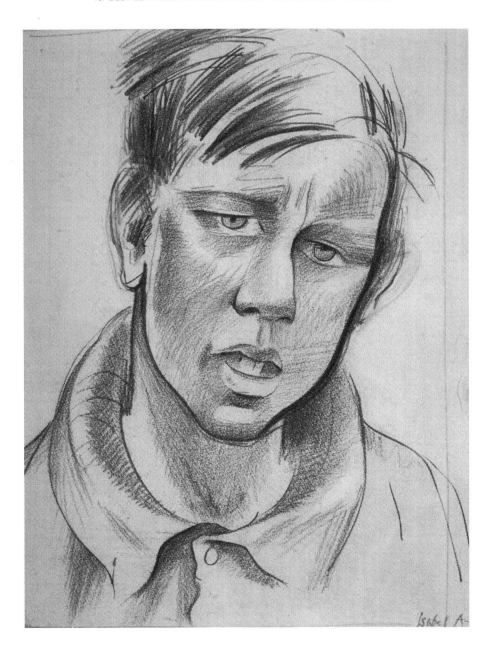

[10] 'Fred, Trealaw', 1943, conté,37 x 27cm. Fred looks about fourteen, old enough to start work in the pit. Other than mining, the main alternatives for a boy of his age in the Rhondda was shop work as a delivery boy. Only if his family could afford to go without his wages would he be able to continue in school. BL Coombes' family had a small farm to run but his son Peter still became a miner.

[11] 'Joan', c1943, pencil, 25 x 20cm. The drawing of serious, dark-eyed teenager Joan stands out as one of the most beautiful of Isabel's portraits of children.

[12] 'Terry, Blaencwm', 1943, pencil, 30 x 22cm. Isabel saw the children she drew with an objective eye as well as humane appreciation of each individual, neither sentimental nor caricaturing. She captures Terry's worried, downward gaze, his layered woollens and his pudding-bowl haircut.

[13] Young girl (unnamed), Rhondda, c1943, pencil, 36 x 26 cm. The intensity of this sketch of a girl recalls Augustus John's drawings of his own children.

[14] *'Graham, Evacuee from Swansea', 1943, pencil, 36 x 27cm. Many children were evacuated from the cities to the Rhondda valleys during the Second World War. Graham may have been sent away from Swansea after the Blitz of 1941, when 230 people were killed in three nights of bombing. Isabel's drawing captures the detail of his school uniform and the knit of his balaclava but still conveys sadness and isolation in his long face and dark, downcast eyes.*

Cultural Institute
Sefydliad Diwylliannol

Swansea University
Prifysgol Abertawe

Championing arts and culture for all, nurturing partnerships, enhancing student experience.

The Cultural Institute is a vibrant, welcoming and inclusive centre within the Faculty of Humanities and Social Sciences at Swansea University.

Our mission is threefold: to champion arts and culture for all, from our staff, students and alumni to schools and communities across Wales and beyond; to nurture collaborations with cultural, literary and publishing partners locally, nationally and internationally; and to enhance the student experience through a wide range of internship opportunities for undergraduates and postgraduates.

From the Swansea University Dylan Thomas Prize, to our literary salon series and special events, educational programmes including a human rights focused poetry project for key stage 3, cross art workshops for key stage 2, and a new, free to attend children's literature festival, we celebrate and promote creativity, imagination, discussion and debate as integral to our wellbeing and shaping us as citizens of the world.

Please do get in touch if you'd like to work with us or have any questions about any of our projects.

www.swansea.ac.uk/cultural-institute | cultural-institute@swansea.ac.uk

 @Culture_SwanUni

 /CultureSwanUni

 @culture_swanuni

 @cultureswanuni

WREXHAM, CAPITAL OF WELSHNESS: A QUILT V HOLLYWOOD

CHRIS MOSS' TRAVEL WRITING FOCUSES
ON 'UNDERTOURISTED' PLACES

Photographs by the author

Pistyll Rhaeadr and Wrexham steeple,
Snowdon's mountain without its people,
Overton yew trees, St Winefride's well,
Llangollen bridge and Gresford bells.
     Anon (probably a tourist), late eighteenth century

DEMOLITION HAS HAD A BALL IN WREXHAM, ERASING STRUCTURES
in many styles from many eras. The Victorian St Mark's church, which had
a two-hundred-foot spire, was destroyed in 1959. The 1909 Hippodrome
theatre/cinema, gutted by a fire in 2008, has gone. A Brutalist police station
was pulled down in 2020. A mock Tudor Vegetable Market was demolished
to make way for a BHS, now also extinct. Manchester, Birmingham and
Yorkshire Squares, where trading in textiles, hardware and leather from those
respective regions took place, have disappeared. Some nineteenth century
sources refer to Sheffield and Bradford Squares. In 2022, the old Rhosddu
vicarage was removed. At the time of writing, an eighteenth century Moreton
pub – despite local protests – is scheduled to make way for housing. The

150-stall open air market (formerly a Beast Market) was closed to make way for a Tesco. Fewer than half the stalls moved to a new space which was in turn usurped by Asda and subsequently Eagles Meadow, a Spanish Steps-themed shopping centre. The mall ousting the mart was merely the latest repurposing. Old OS maps show a Horse Repository at the site. A US army division parked its cars there. All towns have ghost-buildings. Augmented Reality might one day make past layers simultaneously viewable.

When you visit a lot of UK towns, as I do for my *Guardian* column, 'Where Tourists Seldom Tread', you're faced with losses, negatives, vacancies. Heritage – in particular industrial and commercial buildings – has been erased. In its place are empty shops and run-down public spaces. As, wherever you happen to be, another Amazon van whizzes by, the regulation duo of scrawny drug-users squabble and wail, and the only 'shoppers' seem to be sheltering from the world in a grimy branch of Costa or Nero, it's natural to become disheartened – even despairing. It's too easy, prompted by cyclical, unnuanced news reports of empty high streets, pub closures and social inequality, to let your perspective enter a parallel downward spiral: all's grim, the good days are over, this town is doomed, same as all the others.

In 2022, I started to scribble my short articles, because mass tourism has turned many cities, as well as well-preserved towns and villages into hellholes, their grade I Tudor houses, quirky museums and auteur eateries mobbed by extraordinary numbers of visitors. After the lockdowns, we definitely entered the era of the Overtourist: a consumer-oriented, smartphone-zapping, social-sharing drone, most at home pouting in a crowd – ticking off travel destinations 'before they die', presumably because the pandemic made that more of a likelihood.

The sole purpose of my column is to make people spend their leisure time in Undertouristed places. To date, I've filed sixty towns, and am reworking around half that number into book chapters. Let me clarify: my purpose is not ironic, nor is it to go there 'so you don't have to'. I sincerely, profoundly believe every place is interesting – and only a dull mind allied to a lack of information causes us to think otherwise.

Wrexham was a shoo-in. The capital of north Wales, the home of Welsh football and the antithesis of packaged-tourism Wales, it screamed and chanted to be visited.

*

General Market, built in 1879 as Butter Market.

Walking around central Wrexham in July 2024, I step over and around building sites. Regeneration is rife; city status – granted in 2022 at the fourth time of asking – appears to have attracted investment. The old commercial core – High Street, Town Hill and Abbot Street – is a clamorous, obstacle-strewn mess of machines and men at work. The energy is palpable. You can't see shuttered shops for the dust.

Given the history of absences, I'm on the lookout for old things, allusive survivors. Bank Street, an alleyway, feels like a secret. Marubbi's Temperance Bar, opened in 1896 (warm Vimto is its speciality), stands across a tiny square from a jewellers opened in 1932. The General Market (formerly the Butter Market, for dairy produce), built in 1879 in the area's famous Ruabon brick, faces a Meat Market. Workmen are hammering and hewing inside both sites; the facades are quietly grand. A row of seventeenth century timber-framed shops on Chester Street – originally cottages – look semi-rural and refined.

I sometimes wonder if Wales hasn't been too heedful of Gerald's famous prescription – issued principally to himself – that it's necessary to 'give celebrity to a cottage' to avoid disappointing those who come looking for palaces and temples. St Giles' church floors anyone who makes it to Wrexham. Tall, voluminous, richly decorated, built in Cefn sandstone – moodily soot-darkened (perhaps the sandblasters can be kept at bay) – it stands mighty and magnificent on the top of Town Hill. The ornate wrought-iron gates to the churchyard lie at the end of a side street off the main shopping drag. One minute: New Look, Nationwide, Chequer's Cocktail Bar and Figo's Pizza Palace. The next: glory and death, art and eternal life. I rest on a bench. British towns are short on both tranquillity and fee-free places to sit; St Giles' churchyard is soothing and solitary-friendly.

Entombed nearby are the remains of Elihu Yale – misspelled Eliugh – of university fame. His name is celebrated in the local Wetherspoons. This chain follows the same formula everywhere: buy a building that would impress Pevsner; rename it after a local legend; serve cheap ale at all hours and offer catering along pub-grub lines. No music. No familiar bar staff. No meetings with strangers. American-born Yale was governor-president of the British East India Company in Madras (present-day Chennai) and traded in slaves. Wetherspoons doesn't care about the details.

St Giles' would impress in a carefully conserved Italian city. In Wrexham it is immense, and a powerful reminder that the town was Wales' largest in the seventeenth and eighteenth centuries. There are further hints of ecclesiastical prominence. The two Gothic standouts are the Roman Catholic cathedral by Edward Welby Pugin (his only building in Wales) and the

Ruabon redbrick Presbyterian church by William Beddoes Rees, with its distinctive belltower. A glassy Methodist church on Regent Street might seem at first glance lost – it's sited above a row of shops – but strikes me as thoroughly Modern. Shall I buy a pasty or think about God?

A grand High Victorian Gothic archway on Hope Street leads nowhere. Commissioned by Scottish-born engineer, William Low, it was the turnstiled entrance to the Art Treasures & Industrial Exhibition of North Wales, held in 1876. Similar art shows were mounted in Dublin and Manchester to advertise local wealth and cultural sophistication. One highlight was made locally: a quilt by military master tailor, James Williams (c1818–1895) of 8, College Street, Wrexham. The pieced composition depicts biblical scenes – Adam naming the animals, Jonah and the Whale, Noah's Ark with a dove bearing an olive branch, Cain and Abel – as well as Telford's Menai Suspension Bridge, a Chinese pagoda, and Cefn Viaduct, complete with a crossing steam train. Where the glass and iron exhibition hall once stood is now parking bays and the backsides of shops. A relief and plaque inside the arch remind us that Low, who had a wealth of experience in mining, drew the first plans for a Channel tunnel to France; it didn't get beyond geological studies but Low's twin-bore concept was adopted in the eventual Channel tunnel.

The Soames Brewery Chimney – erected in 1894 – stands stranded at the foot of Yorke Street. Once our working-class towns were forests of chimneys. The few remaining are, if not beautiful, bracing and suggestive; they soar away from the flat boxes and twisted road networks of now. The Nag's Head, nearby, started brewing here in the 1830s, and was later used as a boardroom when Soames' was merged into the Border Breweries.

Drink has long been important in Wrexham. 'Lager Town' was its nickname for years, adopted as the handle for CB radio users. At one time there were nineteen breweries. In his richly detailed memoir-cum-travelogue *Real Wrexham* (Seren, 2007), Grahame Davies refers to the Cymdeithas Owain Cyfeiliog literary society which used to meet at the Belmont Hotel, a local

Soames Brewery Chimney, Grade II listed, on Tuttle Street.

pub. The only work to survive by Owain Cyfeiliog aka Owain ap Gruffud ap Maredudd (c1130–1197) is 'Owain's Drinking-horn'. Regarded as a classic, it toasts bravery, camaraderie and the dead.

> Fill the horn with foaming liquor,
> Fill it up my boy, be quicker;
> Hence away, despair and sorrow!
> Time enough to sigh to-morrow.
> Let the brimming goblet smile,
> And Ednyfed's cares beguile*

According to George Borrow, who travelled through Wales in 1854, the only Welsh Wrexham inhabitants had was 'Cwrw da' [good beer].

I visited a dozen pubs, and there were another dozen I might have tried. Town pubs each have their own atmosphere, hanging like a second sign over the doorway: The Heavy Drinkers; The Would-Be Bohemians; The Conspirers; The Lost and Lonely. I'm not a lager drinker but I made an exception. In 1882, two German-born entrepreneurs based in Manchester, Ivan Levinstein and Otto Isler, decide to try to recreate the lager taste they were missing in their adopted homeland of tepid bitter and flat mild. They chose Wrexham so that they could make use of the River Gwenfro's fresh water and exploit its hillsides to ease construction of underground cellars where fermenting ale could be insulated from external heat. Pilsner-style lager requires a cold environment. The temperature proved harder to control than they expected and the beer was tainted. The initial business failed but another German immigrant, Robert Graesser – who had established a chemical works at Acrefair, Denbighshire – came up with a solution using mechanical refrigeration. As locals were used to warmer, darker ale, the Wrexham Lager Brewing Company focused on London and the export market. Wrexham Lager was sent to Australia, Bermuda, Brazil, Ceylon and China and drunk on ocean liners operated by the White Star Line – including *The Titanic*. When Lord Kitchener entered the city of Khartoum in Sudan, in 1898, a stock of Wrexham Lager was found in the deceased General Gordon's palace.

The only architectural vestige of the enterprise is a somewhat Tyrolean building on Central Road, now home to a financial advice firm. The Wrexham Lager brand was reborn in 2011. I had a bottle at the Tŷ Pawb market, along with a beef and ale pie and also a pint of draft with a chicken bhuna at the Indian restaurant, IJazz. I can vouch for its authentic lagerness: refreshing, acidic, forgettable. It always was. That's why the local Temperance Society approved: 'The Wrexham Lager Brewery has been successful in producing a light, pilsner lager, which not only refreshes, but acts as a tonic in cases of weak digestion and is almost non-intoxicating.'

*

My sense of the frontier between my homeland of Lancashire/Cheshire and north Wales was largely defined when I was very small and was taken on holiday to Rhyl, Colwyn Bay, Prestatyn and Llandudno. Runcorn Bridge was 'the border', as far as I was concerned. Wales was less exotic than exciting, connected principally with the sea, beaches, chocolate milk and chalets. The Ll-words were a small and inconsequential joke. I was not yet ten, but my narrow view of Cymru was similar to that of the adults ferrying me: a land of leisure, consumption, rest and general unseriousness. Centuries of disrespect, verging on disdain, have led to a chasmal lack of imagination in the English attitude to its ancient, quasi-foreign neighbour – not so different in essence to the ignorance and arrogance shown by the USA for Mexico and the rest of América [sic].

Many English people think of Wales through a filter of cliché and condescension. Rugby and choirs. Green hills and rundown resorts. One motorway. Coal: gone. Steel: going. The language: revived, but insecure. There's also a fey Arthurian–Merlinian slant, that muddles easily with Dylan Thomas' surrealism.

Wrexham is unpackaged Wales. It is actually closer to my childhood village of Burtonwood than Lancaster, our county town. It is an archetypal border town, lying east of parts of England and Offa's Dyke. It even has a border inside it. Wrexham Abbott was owned by the abbeys. Wrexham Regis vaunted its allegiance to the Crown. The boundary between the ancient townships can still be traced along Abbot Street, the banks of the River Clywedog and the railways. It is seen, from both sides of the frontier, as the poor piggy in the middle of Shrewsbury and Chester. It stands alone, with fields on all sides, and hills and mountains to cross to reach other Welsh conurbations. From Cardiff it is farther by train than London. I drove the A483 Swansea to Manchester road many times when living in Laugharne a decade ago. I have taken short breaks in Harlech, Shropshire, Welshpool. I didn't give Wrexham a first thought. It is the kind of workaday, ex-industrial place we all bypass. The Welsh call rice and chips 'half and half'. It always sounded like a poor choice to me. I think I thought of Wrexham as half and half, diluted, unde-cided, grey-coloured. If only there had been a checkpoint....

In *Border Country* (1960), Raymond Williams evokes the transformation of Wales by the railway. Scattered homesteads became clusters. The novel, set in the Fifties with flashbacks to two decades earlier, hints at how the car will reorder the world again, in tandem with industrial decline and social changes. Wrexham is an archetypal border town, in the vanguard of change, under constant pressure from England, floating freely away from deep, rural Wales and barely connected to the summery fictions of the seaside.

It was once an industrial crucible. There were coal and iron ore in Ponciau, Rhos and Llwyn Einion, limestone quarries at Minera, charcoal from the woods around Coedpoeth and waterpower from the Clywedog. By the late eighteenth century, the Bersham ironworks – recently taken over by Cumbrian John 'Iron Mad' Wilkinson – ran night and day, turning out state-of-the-art cannon parts and steam engine cylinders. Wilkinson sank his own coal mines and expanded operations to Brymbo Steel Works. Legends whirled around him: he discovered coal tar, and coal gas; he founded Wilkinson's Sword; he built the iron bridge in Shropshire. None were true but he was immense to the locals who worked for him and the many thousands who clocked on in later generations.

Gresford is an ancient settlement. One of the yew trees in the church-yard of All Saints is fifteen hundred years old. Yews were sacred to the Celts. In 1908, a Roman altar was discovered in the church. It was dedicated to

Nemesis, the goddess of fate. She was the daughter of Erebus, king of the underworld, and his sister Nyx, goddess of the night, and the granddaughter of Chaos. Myth would hit hard against rock. Gresford Colliery began to produce coal in 1911. By 1934, the workforce had grown to 2200, many from the purpose-built Garden Village, but with workers drawn from all the surrounding villages. On Saturday 22 September, 1934, five hundred men were on nights – more than the usual number as they were putting in an extra shift to have the Sunday off to watch the derby between Wrexham and Tranmere.

At eight minutes past two, a spark ignited a build-up of gas, and an explosion ripped through the Dennis section of the mine, causing a fire. Those close by were killed instantly. Others quickly succumbed to carbon monoxide released by the blast. Six managed to escape, but 261 men were killed. Miners and rescue workers were soon to respond, but the fire was out of control and six rescuers were killed. They decided the only course of action was to seal off the entire section and leave their comrades in a mass grave more than two thousand feet down. It was the second worst mining disaster in Welsh history, after the 1913 Senghenydd explosion which killed 439 miners and a rescuer. Only eleven bodies (eight miners and the three rescue men) were ever recovered. A controversial inquiry into the disaster did not conclusively identify a cause, though failures in safety procedures, ineffective ventilation and poor mine management were contributory factors.

A pitwheel on a small patch of lawn beside the Gresford Colliery Sports and Social Club commemorates the tragedy. A memorial book in the magnificent church lists the dead: many Griffiths, Evanses and Thomases, three separate John Williamses and four Thomas Joneses. A folk music broadside honours the miners' memory, possibly penned by rescue team leader, John Charles Williams; Ewan McColl recorded a version of it in 1957.** As the bodies were being brought out, the colliery band was at the pithead playing to soothe the spirits of the wives, children and friends. One tune they played was 'How Sweet the Name of Jesus Sounds in a Believer's Ear', written by DH Lawrence's great-grandfather. The Albion Band set the words of the broadside to the hymn on their 1978 album *Rise Up to the Sun*. In September 2024, a new community opera, *Gresford: Up From Underground*, was premiered at St Asaph Cathedral. Grahame Davies' libretto – which incorporates the broadside – emphatically contrasts the fame of the Seven Wonders of Wales (all found in the north) – including the bells at All Saints – with the relative amnesia that has re-buried the victims of the Gresford disaster:

Caiff rhai eu cadw allan	Some places don't get noticed.
a rhai eu cadw i lawr.	Some people don't get seen.
Ni sonnwyd am rai pethau gynt.	Some subjects don't get mentioned now.
Ni sonnir am rai nawr.	And some have never been.
Rhai straeon ni adroddwyd.	Some tales just get forgotten.
Rhai eraill aeth dros go'.	And some are never told.
Rhai straeon sy'n rhy boenus.	Some stories are too searing.
Rhai clustiau sydd dan glo.	Some hearers are too cold.

Industry and violence are never far apart. Pill boxes and remnants of random defensive structures, festooned with vegetation, litter the area chosen for Wrexham's Royal Ordnance Factory. Rail networks and a ready supply of labour made it a natural choice for a factory producing cordite for shells. Part of the area was used subsequently to build the UK's second largest industrial estate and largest prison, HMP Berwyn.

*

Visitors to Wrexham can't ignore football, try as they may. The Racecourse Ground looms above General Station. Manager Phil Parkinson's face is daubed on a fence outside the Turf pub. Street art idolising striker Paul Mullin covers the gable wall of the Fat Boar. Shop windows showcase footy-themed T-shirts. A painting of Rob McElhenney in the style of Kate Winslet's nude drawing, in the 1997 movie *Titanic*, hangs at the Tŷ Pawb

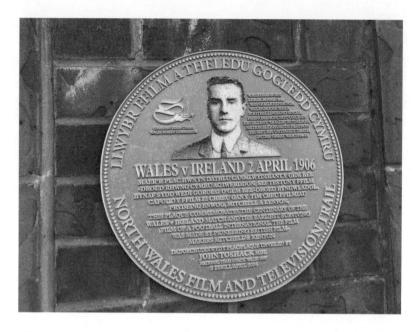

Plaque on wall outside Wrexham AFC's Racecourse stadium commemorates the centenary of the Wales v Ireland match of 2 April, 1906, the 'earliest surviving film of a football international' (though the BFI claims a 1905 film of England v Ireland, also by Mitchell and Kenyon, is the oldest).

gallery. It was given to him, on his forty-seventh birthday, by Wrexham AFC co-owner, Ryan Reynolds. Amid the road tearing-up and building work, hoardings on Henblas Street declare that the Memorial Parc Ryan Rodney Reynolds is under construction – apparently a gift from McElhenney to Reynolds for *his* forty-seventh birthday. This is where the Hippodrome cinema used to stand.

The Disney+ series, *Welcome to Wrexham*, is unwatchable, at least for a neutral. It is not about football. It isn't really about Wrexham. It's about two celebrities having heaps of bro-fun by means of the commodification of football and its supporters. Vast amounts of lip service have been paid to the show, including by erudite locals, perhaps out of gratitude for 'putting Wrexham on the map' as well as reviving the ambitions of the long struggling, now twice promoted club. But I can't shake off the feeling that the relationship, for all its putative positives, is ironic and whimsical. There's plenty of circumstantial evidence. *Deadpool* is a parody of a Marvel super-hero. The TV and money-focused English football league is a parody of sport. The American celebrities are parodies of genuine football fans. Wrexham's football story is useful as a parodical stunt. If you want to think about how Americans see Wales, then think about how you see America. Their telescope is held the other way round; Wrexham is a quaint or quirky dot in the green-grey landscape, faraway.

As Terry Eagleton wrote in *The Guardian* in 2010, 'Modern societies deny men and women the experience of solidarity, which football provides to the point of collective delirium.' As carnival, church, Roman circus and amphitheatre, football touches many tender scars in the human soul. It triggers so much that has been lost, shrivelled, debauched, ridiculed. Eagleton's chief argument is that all this wizardry is at the service of capitalism and populism. 'Football these days is the opium of the people, not to speak of their crack cocaine.... Nobody serious about political change can shirk the fact that the game has to be abolished.'

Or reformed. Or amateurised. Or something. The prominence of football across the UK is a devastating sign of a national lack of hope, a fixation with a mono-sport, to go with the mono-agriculture, mono-high streets, mono-politics. Headlines like 'Club Necaxa's backers purchased 5% of Wrexham AFC in April 2024 and both owners, in turn, purchased a minority stake in Club Necaxa' freak me out for their sheer surreality. And I don't support Wrexham.

But the town's footballing past is woven into so much else. For most of its history, Wrexham was one of only four Welsh clubs in the English league. It kicked above its weight in cup encounters, beating First Division titans Newcastle in 1978 and Arsenal in 1992. Thanks to successes in the Welsh Cup, it routinely qualified for the European Cup Winners' cup. The club, formed in 1872, is one of the oldest in Wales. The Racecourse was a major venue for soccer internationals until Cardiff's Millennium Stadium supplanted it.

Mitchell and Kenyon, the Blackburn moving picture pioneers, shot one of the oldest international football encounters when they filmed Wales v Ireland in 1906 at the Racecourse. Four of the eight goals scored (in a 4–4 draw) were recorded for posterity. Claims that this is the oldest extant soccer film in the world are wide of the mark, but they may have captured the first football injury on film, when an Irish striker collapses after what looks like a pulled hamstring in his right leg.

Fat Boar pub: giant mural of Wrexham's star striker Paul Mullin on the gable end, unveiled in summer 2023.

Historically, working-class towns turned to football for respite, solidarity, a laugh, a drink. Today the game's influence is more complicated. On a search engine, club names elide those of towns. Google Stoke, Wigan or Wrexham, and football tables come up before news, culture, services, history. Local newspapers, which are almost uniformly awful, prioritise tittle-tattle about the local team over anything as banal as investment, new buildings or pressing social issues.

Wrexham football is valuable only as part of the town's story. The museum is being refurbished to house a football exhibition. Perhaps the curators can reclaim the beautiful quilt – currently at St Ffagans, Cardiff – to remind visitors that all history is patches and strands.

*

Waiting for the train home on the platform at Wrexham General, I noticed the word 'hiraeth' on a window. It was painted there by artist Sophia Leadill as part of an artist-in-residence project,*** according to a sign on the neighbouring door – which was locked. Somewhere between hiraeth's grief and longing and the aggressive hype of the football-crazed present, lies a more interesting, time-skewing story of a town morphing into a city, of ruins mingled with regeneration, of lager fantasies and vaulting church dreams, of dead miners and opera (and folk) singers. In 1998, Wrexham offered itself as home for the new National Assembly for Wales. But Cardiff got the Senedd, along with everything else. Wrexham and its region were not chosen as sites for the founding constituent colleges of the University of Wales during the latter decades of the nineteenth century. There is no National Museum outreach in the town. The BBC chose Bangor for its north Wales headquarters despite the far larger population in the north-east.

At the 2007 National Eisteddfod in Mold, Flintshire, the late historian John Davies observed, 'There is a tendency – in the south in particular, but also perhaps in the north-west – to consider the north-east to be a rather detached part of Wales, or, indeed, to be more of an adjunct of Merseyside than an integral part of the Welsh nation.... The region has not had its share of Welsh institutions, not because it is an unsuitable place in which to locate such institutions, but because we in the rest of Wales have connived in the region's marginalisation.'****

He pointed out that the first written evidence of any area of Wales is

Tacitus' account of the Roman attack upon the Deceangli, who lived between the Dee and the Clwyd. The large military camp discovered at Rhyn Park in 1975 indicates the scale of the Roman preparations and the degree of resistance they were expecting.

Davies added:

> The Eliseg pillar in Llangollen; the constant toing and froing between the Kingdoms of Wales and England in this part of the world during the Middle Ages which helped define what we today know as modern Wales; the home of Owain Glyndwr – this all before even thinking of the huge role the area and its people played over the last five hundred years.

Artwork by Sophie Leadhill at waiting room, platform 3 of Wrexham General Station, relating to the project 'Hiraeth – Belonging Across Borders'; Leadill worked with KIM Inspire, The Wallich, Housing Justice and a local refugee group.

Borderlands are intriguing, porous, tense, contested; Glyndwr was most fully alive waging war on the Gwynedd/Salop fringes. Wrexham, where mountain meets plain, stone abuts brick, accents and languages merge and meet, is hard to define, to summarise, to pin down. Borderland vagueness is sometimes perceived as non-place. Wrexonians are not considered as being as Welsh as West Walians, or North Walians, or even South Walians, as if distance from England or proximity to the sea or to the recently crowned capital city intensifies nationhood. But Wales was birthed at and from and through its border – in acts of resistance, bloody battles, hillforts and the earthwork of Offa's Dyke. Wrexham can't be disappeared by those who disdain its chronic in-betweenness any more than it can by those who swing the wrecking ball.

Notes
* https://allpoetry.com/Hirlas-Owain,-Or,-The-Drinking-Horn-Of-Owen
**https://mainlynorfolk.info/ewan.maccoll/songs/thegresforddisaster.html#ewanmaccoll
***https://www.google.co.uk/books/edition/A_Marginalised_Region/rYE9p01vBPMC?hl=en&gbpv=1
****https://www.sophialeadill.co.uk/project-cat/decor/

For three years, regular *NWR* writer **Chris Moss** has been filing a column on offbeat tourist destinations for *The Guardian*'s Travel pages. He's currently working on a book-length collection – here's his dispatch on Wrexham.

Wrexham is bidding to be the UK City of Culture for 2029, having missed out to Bradford for 2022. An public art trail of new murals and artworks is in train: wrecsam2029.wales/wrecsam-uk-city-of-culture-bid-2029-wrexham-public-art-trail/

New and prize-listed titles from **Firefly Press**

£9.99
ISBN 9781915444318

Shortlisted for the Yoto Carnegie Medal
for Writing 2025

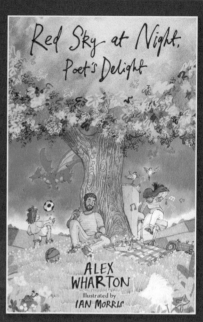

£6.99
ISBN 9781915444356

Longlisted for the Jhalak Children's & Young
Adult Prize 2025

£8.99
ISBN 9781915444844

'Smart, funny, heartbreaking. This is *Catcher
in The Rye* for south Wales.' Nicola Davies

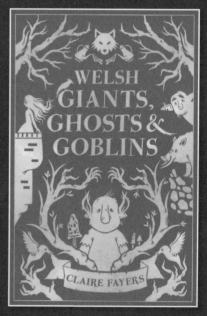

£10.99
ISBN 9781915444707

Shortlisted for the Tir na n-Og 2025

PRISONERS, HEROES, AMNESIA AND 'HOUSEWIFISATION'

RYOTA NISHI ON THE HISTORY OF FEMALE MINERS, AND THE ROLE OF
THEIR EXPERIENCE DURING PIT CLOSURE IN JAPAN, WALES AND THE UK

Translation revision by Gwen Davies

THE YEARS 2024 AND 2025 MARKED TWO ANNIVERSARIES OF
significant miners' strikes in the UK: the fiftieth anniversary of the 1974
strike and the fortieth anniversary of the 1984–1985 strike. Both collec-
tively represent a pivotal moment in the decline of the UK's coal industry.
Four decades after the mass pit closures under Thatcher, the pervasive and
enduring impact of the coal industry and its decline persists in and beyond
those former mining regions. Indeed, its history resonates with that of
mining communities worldwide, and in particular, in Japan. In Britain
and specifically Wales, these effects encompass a range of socio-economic
concerns, including elevated unemployment rates and a shrinking workforce, as well as environmental issues such as an increased risk of landslides
at slag heaps during heavy rainfall. Furthermore, these factors are not
exclusive to quantitative, measurable, subjects; they are also observed in
qualitative socio-cultural dynamics, such as long-term shifts in the culture
and collective mind-set cultivated in coal communities. In this sense, the
legacy, or 'after-life', of coal has not been entirely erased, and its longstand-
ing after-life is not limited to the UK; it can be observed in many former
coalfields globally.

This article focuses on women's experience, and explores its meaning during pit closure in both the UK (including Wales), and Japan, as well as its significance today.

Women's experience of 'housewifisation' and its repercussions in the struggle against pit closure in the UK

One illustrative example of the impact of the coal industry, and its decline, on the lives and culture of coalfield communities, is the experience of coalfield women. A comprehensive and long-term examination of historical evidence has yet to be conducted in sufficient depth to demonstrate the conditions experienced by women in different times and situations, ranging from those who engaged in underground coal mining during the early years of the British coal mining industry, to those who endured hardship during the pit closure in the late twentieth century. Nevertheless, there are a number of notable researchers engaged in such experience. In *Women and the Miners' Strike, 1984–1985*, for instance, Sutcliffe-Braithwaite and Thomlinson employ a multifaceted approach to shed light on the diverse experience of coalfield women during the strike, including women's support movements whose story has hitherto been told in 'heroic mode' (Sutcliffe-Braithwaite and Thomlinson, p2). To this end, they integrated an analysis of oral life histories of over one hundred women in the coalfields of England, Scotland, and Wales, together with media coverage and sociological studies. Their laborious research successfully delineates the diversity of women's experience, including that of those who actively engaged in support groups, not only creating an 'alternative welfare system' to support striking miners and their families, but also constructing a 'moral economy that demanded miners and their families... strike [in order] to honour the miners of the past, and to defend the communities of the future' (p3), as well as exploring the motivations of those who didn't engage in the movement.

It is quite striking, however, that, in these accounts, 'the miner of the past' here does not seem to include those women who had actually themselves worked in the pit until their underground labour was prohibited in the mid-nineteenth century. In her seminal work, *Women in Welsh Coal Mining – Tip Girls at Work in a Men's World*, Norena Shopland undertakes a meticulous endeavour to restore the history of women who worked at coalmines. In order to illuminate their circumstances, and particularly that of 'tip girls' in Wales from the late eighteenth to the mid twentieth century, Shopland conducts a thorough study of various types of historical document, including accidental death records, newspaper coverage, and census data. While the proportion of women employed in the coal industry was relatively low in comparison to that of men, there were nevertheless a number of women and girls engaged in various types of work within collieries. Many of them engaged in underground mining, transporting excavated coal to the surface until the mid-nineteenth century, when the practice was prohibited. Thereafter, the majority gradually transitioned to surface labour at the pit bank. However, the advent of mechanisation and the ascendancy of patriarchal norms compelled the majority of them to move, during the late eighteenth and nineteenth centuries, from their original roles as working women to those of miners' wives. Despite their historical presence and significance within the coal mining industry, the struggle of these women labourers seemingly still escapes collective memory, even among the women's support groups of the 1984–1985 strike. It is possible that the history of 'tip girls' and other women who laboured in the coal industry against both patriarchal and capitalist oppression, might have potentially empowered women's activism during the strike; however, their stories appear to have been completely forgotten. The reasons for this apparent collective amnesia are not immediately clear. However, a deeper understanding of the historical processes of 'housewifisation' and its long-term effects may offer some insight.

The most significant legislative effort to prohibit women from working underground, turning them into housewives, was the *Mines and Collieries Act 1842*, which made illegal the employment in underground mines of all boys under the age of ten and all women of any age. Nevertheless, a considerable number of women continued to work underground over subsequent decades, due to the insufficient number of inspectors of mines, which resulted in 'the law in many places' being 'simply ignored' (Shopland, p59). Consequently, it required the exertion of considerable effort, over a period exceeding a century, to drive these women out of the pit and into domestic roles. This was characterised by a relentless focus on a perceived lack of femininity, the 'unsexing' of women and aspersions about their apparent immorality (Shopland, p69-70), which, based on patriarchal morality, was designed to blame the prohibition of women's underground work on the women themselves rather than on the harsh working environment. This process should be understood as part of a process of housewifisation rather than a mere domestication of women. The latter term is generally utilised to describe the process of merely integrating women into the domestic sphere, whereas the former is employed to emphasise the process of depriving women of economic independence and a mentality of self-reliance, thereby integrating them into the system of patriarchy. Furthermore, this integration also contributes to the accumulation of capital by forcing women to assume responsibility for the burden of all unpaid domestic labour as well as reproductive labour. In essence, the century-long transformation of female miners into housewives, assigning them to unpaid domestic and reproductive labour, enabled male miners to endure the rigorous labour of the colliery. Consequently, the process of housewifisation of female miners during the nineteenth century can be regarded as some kind of dual-faceted groundwork for the mid-twentieth century miner's wives support group: the transformation of women miners into housewives and the concomitant strengthening of patriarchal structures that normalise women's role as wives.

It is important to note here, however, that being a housewife did not necessarily limit her participation to activism; rather, the broader 'domestic sphere was often a key source of pride, respectability, and identity for working-class women' during the 1984–1985 strike (Sutcliffe-Braithwaite and Thomlinson, p145). There were women within support groups who later admitted to having challenging interactions with feminists who came to the south Wales Valleys to support the strike. It could be argued that the

strong identity of these women as housewives was incompatible with feminist politics, which was predominantly influenced by middle-class values
and a metropolitan perspective. Whatever the intricacies of identity-loyalty,
the process of housewifisation should certainly be more thoroughly examined. It should not be regarded merely as a weakening of coalfield women,
resulting in the loss alone of their economic independence and self-reliance.
Instead, it should be recognised as a process of women gaining self-awareness, which had been cultivated in the mining communities, and which the
prevailing feminist perspective at that time had failed to pay much regard
to. In this respect, the 1984–1985 strike and subsequent pit closures must
be understood as part of a long resilient process of women's acquisition of
self-awareness and empowerment. However, the question of the role of the
experience of women miners, or 'tip girls', in this process remains unresolved.
Further study is necessary to determine the extent to which their experience
contributed to this later process, especially considering that this role appears
to have been erased from collective memory. While I am unable to offer a
definitive answer, I will use the case of Japan to illustrate my points.

**Forms of forced labour in the Japanese coal industry and their unantici-
pated cultural consequences**

The cultural implications of Japanese coal mining and its underground
labour are unique. The image of miners in the UK is, in general, one surrounded by respect: miners who might sometimes seem rough, but who
took pride in their labour and later fought bravely against pit closures. In
contrast, Japanese miners have often been negatively stereotyped as poor,
rough and criminal. This negative impression is partly rooted in the nature
of underground working conditions, which were generally considered to be
so arduous and gruelling that they would not be voluntarily undertaken.
Another source of the dreadful image of collieries is in the historical context
of Japan's coalmining industry.

Japanese mining areas can be divided into three primary regions: the northern coalfields of Hokkaidō Island, the Joban coalfields in the middle of the Japanese mainland, and the coalfields of Kyushu Island in the south. Despite the distinct characteristics and individual histories of each mine within these regions, they all share a comparable historical origin (*Naraku* pt1, ch2). This included some form of forced labour. A notable example is the specialised prison system known as Shuchikan, through which the Japanese government established the indigenous coalmining industry. This system, instituted after the two-decade upheaval of Meiji Restoration in the late nineteenth century, involved the forced labour of convicted individuals, many of whom were political prisoners opposed to the imperialistic regime intent on modernising Japan. The first institution of this kind was established in Tōkyō in 1878, but the majority were concentrated in Hokkaidō, a region that had only recently been incorporated into Japanese territory by expropriating the land of the indigenous Ainu people. The Japanese government's settler colonialism in Hokkaidō necessitated a substantial workforce for infrastructure and agricultural development, railway construction and mining for sulphur and coal, and the Shuchikan system was an indispensable component of this endeavour. This system functioned to drive what Marx termed 'the primitive accumulation of capital' by generating sufficiently cheap and disposable labour to effect the industrialisation of Japan (Kim, p20).

Prior to the advent of government operations, collieries were already regarded as breeding grounds for impoverished vagrants living at the margins of law-abiding respectable society. This negative perception meant that it was difficult to recruit enough workers for the coalmines. It was for this reason that the Shuchikan system was introduced. When Miike coalmine, the largest in Japan (situated in the north-west coast of Kyusyu Island), was brought under the control of the Mitsui Zaibatsu family-run conglomerate in 1889, for instance, 2144 out of 3103 miners were prisoners (*Naraku* pt2, ch3). The Mitsui continued to utilise this system to ensure a big enough workforce up to the advent of innovative mining technology, which demanded a more skilled labour force, and thus the use of prisoners was phased out.

In those smaller or more remote collieries where the Shuchikan system was not introduced, alternative forms of forced labour were utilised. A notable example of this is the Naya Seido (shed system), introduced in the mines of the Chikuho coalfield located in the northern region of Kyushu Island. The Naya Seido can be defined as a form of subcontracting, whereby the proprietor of the coalmine employed a manager known as the Naya Gashira, who in turn subcontracted the managerial work of miners' recruitment, their supervision, and their lives in a company-owned terrace house, which was called Naya [shed]. Naya Seido was disguised as a Japanese traditional apprenticeship common in other manual industries, but in fact was forced labour, binding miners to their employment through debt. This arrangement persisted until the inter-war period, at which point the proprietors of the coalmines accumulated sufficient capital to undertake managerial functions directly, thereby enabling them to employ the miners themselves (Ayukawa, p15).

A notable aspect of this system was its emphasis on the employment of married miners, a practice that was particularly suited to the distinctive Hitosaki working arrangement. Under this system, a married couple was regarded as a fundamental component of the workforce at the coalface, with the husband (Sakiyama) responsible for excavation, and the wife (Atoyama) tasked with the extraction of coal. In the Chikuho coalfield, particularly, there existed numerous small mines where the workforce was organised around the couple as the basic unit under the Naya Seido. The labour in the pit, where men and women literally risked their lives while working almost naked on each other's backs, forged a profound bond between them, transcending or even deviating from, the confines of the patriarchal marriages of the era. It has been documented that not a few women, discontented with their husbands' roles as Sakiyama in the pits, formed alliances with more capable men and subsequently eloped (*Naraku* pt2 ch3). This phenomenon should not be construed as some sort of a social aberration of unrestrained sexuality, but rather as a by-product of brutal working conditions.

However, it should be noted that an ideal of gender equality and equal rights for men and women was not in circulation under the Naya Seido. The principle of equal payment was not attained, because traditional patriarchy normalised the underpayment of women. Women who were exhausted from working in the mines were expected to engage in unpaid domestic and reproductive labour in their own homes, supporting their miner husbands, including back-breaking cleaning and laundry tasks. Nevertheless, these women persevered in their work at the collieries, driven by a spirit of resilience and the belief that their capabilities were equal to those of men, despite facing ridicule and ruthless mocking from men, even from their husbands. One of those women who had worked underground in the early twentieth century said, in an interview conducted in the 1950s, that 'men say that a women's cleverness is eight-tenths of a man's, and they make fun of women, but the pit wouldn't last without women. It is women who actually maintain the central pillar of the pit' (Idegawa, p157). Through this labour and lifestyle, a distinctive sexual ethos emerged, characterised by men and women confronting and competing with each other, thereby fostering a miners' culture that depended on mutual support to survive, despite the prevailing conditions of intense labour-force exploitation.

Mining women's experience of underground labour in the struggle against pit closure in Japan

Notwithstanding the severe exploitation and the negative stereotyping that resulted from the different forms of forced labour implemented by the modernising Japanese government and the Zaibatsu, the coalminers and their community cultivated a distinctive and remarkable culture and spirit. A salient point to be made here, however, is the fact that women had been excluded from this labour and culture twice: two legal bans on women working in coalmines were imposed in 1928 and 1948.

The first exclusion was the prohibition of women from working in mines, implemented in 1928 under the Miners' Labour Assistance Regulation Amendment (Ministry of Home Affairs Order No 30). This development emerged as a consequence of a government-initiated study, prompted by the recognition of the necessity to safeguard workers, from a humanitarian standpoint, following deliberations at the annual International Labour Conference held in Washington, USA, in 1919. However, the process also reflected the government's ambition to expeditiously create the impression of a modern state, encompassing contemporary global gender norms. The profound influence of patriarchal gender ideology constrained the scope of 'protection' to women alone, thereby reinforcing the state's doctrine that women should be exclusively engaged in domestic reproductive labour. This was further compounded by the mechanisation of mining, which rendered the arduous task of coal removal superfluous, resulting in women being compelled to leave their occupations. Consequently, women were expected to become citizens performing a role to support the state by taking on the role of 'mother' to 'produce and bring up the Empire's subjects' and the role of 'housewife' to take full responsibility of the household' (Noyori, p131). With some exceptions (not necessarily minor ones), women who had proudly worked in the pits and competed equally with men were suddenly and systematically deprived of economic independence and a foothold to compete equally with men in the workforce, being instead compelled to become housewives. Women who tried to continue working had to accept illegal devalued wages in smaller mines.

The second exclusion of women was the post-war prohibition of women under the Labour Standards Law of 1947, which also seems to have led to a de facto deterioration in working conditions and wages for women in the small-scale mines. These two bans on women from underground work, while ostensibly aimed at 'protection', were in fact a means of instrumentalisation for the establishment of the modern Japanese state, or alternatively a convenient employment adjustment valve to cope with changing economic circumstances. These processes of exclusion should be understood as the process of housewifisation, which is quite similar to the one that happened in the UK, as we observed in the first section. This prompts the same question as in the first one: What was the role played by the experience of housewifisation among Japanese coalfield women during mass pit closure during the 1960s?

The definitive answer to this question is yet to be determined by further studies; however, critical reflections by the Japanese poet Kazue Morisaki (1927–2022) provide a distinctive illustration of the significance of the experiences of women miners during the period of pit closure.

Kazue Morisaki, a writer–activist, was born into an affluent Japanese family residing in Daegu, a major city in South Korea, during the period of Japanese occupation. She 'returned' to Japan to attend college in the very final moments of the Second World War, and graduated from the Women's College of Fukuoka at the age of twenty-three. In search of an apt language for her own experience of being born in the colony and living in a foreign land which she was supposed to consider her 'homeland', she suddenly found herself afflicted with aphasia-like symptoms. Specifically, she experienced difficulty with the articulation of certain Japanese words, including Onna (woman), Nippon (Japan) and Watashi, the first-person pronoun. This led her to the insight that these commonplace Japanese words did not accurately reflect her personal experiences.

In 1959, Morisaki was invited by her friend Gan Tanigawa, a renowned poet and radical leftist, to relocate with him to a mining town in the Chikuho coalfield, which was experiencing labour disputes. This move marked her involvement in the labour movement at Taisho Colliery in Chikuho. Following the announcement of mass layoffs there to address the colliery's substantial deficit, the trade union responded with widespread strikes. Morisaki's involvement in this labour movement, which was predominantly male, and where women were typically relegated to supporting roles, led her to initiate a series of dialogues with the wives of coal miners. These women, like Morisaki herself, were concerned about their own roles within the movement. In the course of her dialogues with coal miner's wives of her own generation, Morisaki realised that their involvement in this battle was not only a battle against finance capital (which was trying to recover its capital by forcing the coal mine to carry out massive personnel reductions) but also against their husbands and other men who maintained patriarchal attitudes. In order to continue this dual struggle, it was necessary to acquire a language that could oppose both capitalism and patriarchy. However, as long as they remained within the confines of their identity as coal miner's wives, it was impossible to create such a language. Morisaki therefore turned to older women who had experienced underground labour, seeking something that could break the impasse.

Morisaki paid frequent visits to those women, collecting stories of their experience of underground labour and subsequent process of housewifisation, which culminated in her first book, *Makkura* (Pitch-Dark), published in 1959. In her introduction, she depicts her anguish:

> I was looking for something. And I visited many elderly women who had experienced underground labour, because I desperately longed for something that could burn me away, myself who lived like a peculiar worm on the ground of Japan. An old woman plumped herself down in front of me, flinging me, a mayfly, aside. Their manner seemed to reflect what class, ethnicity, and women meant to them. Those elements all together seemed to open up like a rainbow inside her. I entered into the crack in their hearts. (p4)

As Morisaki became acquainted with the lives of these women miners, their distinctive sexual ethos, culture of collaboration on an equal footing and simultaneous solidarity with men, and the miners' culture of mutual care that were briefly described in the previous section, she was profoundly shocked to realise that all of these had been completely forgotten by the time she was involved in the labour movement of the late 1950s and 1960s, and she came to recognise their significance. Without some sort of reverse-conditioning out of the prevailing status of being someone's possession (wife, daughter or mother) it would be impossible to seek a language that could truly represent women's experience and the possibility of an equal relationship with men. Without regaining the miners' culture of mutual equal care, it would be impossible to continue any battle against capitalist exploitation. Morisaki learned that this history of equal collaboration was not fable but a reality that women miners had lived. This belief greatly empowered Morisaki and her contemporary women.

The last coalmines in the Chikuho coalfield closed in 1973, marking the defeat of the coalmining labour movement. However, the insights that Morisaki acquired and which were enriched by her listening to mining women's experience of underground labour and learning from their lives, survive. Her books have been republished in recent years, proving the significance of women colliers. It is left to us today to ourselves endeavour to mine what appears to be residual, to retrieve the buried experience of those who have been excluded and silenced. To fully realise the potential of these women, a potential which has hitherto been only 'a pre-emergence, active and pressing but not yet fully articulated' (Williams, p126).

Works cited
Japanese journal articles and titles are presented in translation

'Control of Miners in Chikuho Coal Mines in the Interwar Period', Ayukawa Nobuo (*The Economic Review {Research and Study: Special Issue}*, Kyoto University Economic Society, vol 12, 1997, pp 10-26).

Hi wo Unda Haha Tachi [*Mothers Who Gave Birth to the Flame of Coal*], Yaduko Idegawa (Kaichosha, 2021).

'A Reflection on Prisoners' Labour in Miike Coalmine', Kwang Nam Kim (*Daigaku Kyoiku Kenkyu*, vol 3, 2020, pp 17-36).

Brittle with Relics: A History of Wales, 1962–97, Richard King (Faber & Faber, 2023).

Kindai Chikuho Tanko ni okeru Josei Roudou to Kazoku [*Women's Labour and the Family in the Modern Chikuho Coalmines : The Concept of the 'Family Wage' and the Formation Process of 'Family Ideology'*], Tomoko Noyori (Otsukishoten, 2010).

'Aspects of Historical Understanding of 'Shuchikan' in Hokkaidō: Dark Tourism and Alterity in the Modern Society', Takenori Komatsu

(*Journal of the Faculty of Economics, Asahikawa University*, vol 79, no 80, 2021, pp 23-40).

Patriarchy and Accumulation on a World Scale: Women in the International Division of Labour, Maria Mies (Bloomsbury Academic, 2022).

Naraku no Kamigami: Tanko Rodo Seishinshi [*Gods in the Abyss: A History of the Spirit of Coal Miners*], Kazue Morisaki (e-book edition: Heibonsha, 1996).

Makkura [*The Pitch-Dark*], Kazue Morisaki (Riron-Sha, 1961).

'Perspective Chapter: The Japanese Coal Mining Industry Reconsidered – From Mechanised Longwall Mining to Carbon Dioxide Capture and Storage', Tomoki Shimanishi et al in *Recent Advances for Coal Energy in the Twenty-first Century*, Yongseung Yun (IntechOpen, 7 February, 2024. Crossref, doi:10.5772/intechopen.111816).

Women in Welsh Coal Mining Tip Girls at Work in a Men's World, Norena Shopland (Pen & Sword History, 2023).

Women and the Miners' Strike, 1984–1985, Florence Sutcliffe-Braithwaite and Natalie Thomlinson (Oxford University Press, 2023).

Marxism and Literature, Raymond Williams (Oxford University Press, 1977).

Ryota Nishi is an associate professor at Chuo University in Tōkyō. His original academic field of interest was (and still is) postcolonial theory. However, after the Great East Japan Earthquake of 11 March, 2011 and the subsequent severe accidents at the Fukushima nuclear power plants, he began to research the relationship between and representations of energy industries and workers. Since then, he has studied labour movements in the coalfield and how they were represented. He is also interested in other fields in relation to this subject, including the historical analysis of women's activism in coalfields, discourses of ecology, migration and the movement of peoples, and the theoretical analysis of labour. Welsh writing in English is also included in his interests: he translated Ron Berry's story 'Time Spent' into Japanese.

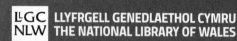

LLYFRGELL GENEDLAETHOL CYMRU
THE NATIONAL LIBRARY OF WALES

ARDDANGOSFA YN ARCHWILIO'R MYTH GYDA PETER LORD

AN EXHIBITION EXPLORING THE MYTH WITH PETER LORD

'DIM CELF GYMREIG'

'NO WELSH ART'

Edward Owen Pentbos, Hunan-bortread/Self-portrait, 1732

16.11.2024 – 13.09.2025

Noddir gan
Lywodraeth Cymru
Sponsored by
Welsh Government

NO WELSH ART?

JOHN BARNIE SURVEYS A LIFE'S WORK CHALLENGING
STEREOTYPES OF THE VISUAL ARTS BY ART HISTORIAN PETER LORD
AT THE NATIONAL LIBRARY OF WALES

'Dim Celf Gymreig': Arddangosfa yn Archwilio'r Myth gyda Peter Lord / 'No
Welsh Art': An Exhibition Exploring the Myth with Peter Lord
National Library of Wales, 16 November, 2024–6 September, 2025

THE TITLE OF THIS EXHIBITION IS TAKEN FROM AN OBSERVATION MADE
in 1950 by Llewelyn Wyn Griffith: 'So much for the past. No patron, no
critic, therefore no painter, no sculptor, no Welsh art. It is as simple as that.'
At the time, Griffith was Chair of the Welsh Committee of the Arts Council
of Great Britain and it must have seemed that he knew what he was talking
about. In fact, there is no better example of what Australians call 'cultural
cringe', because Griffith was echoing the prevailing metropolitan view. The
brochure accompanying the exhibition quotes the English art critic David
Bell, who wrote a few years later: 'A small peasant people like the Welsh does
not, cannot provide the conditions in which the fine arts flourish… on any but
an elementary level.' This from his book *The Artist in Wales* (Harrap, 1957).

Ironically, it was another Englishman, Peter Lord, who was instrumental
in giving the lie to this dreary libel. When he came to live in Ceredigion in
1974 it was primarily as an artist, but over the years he became interested
in the phenomenon of Welsh art and began to collect paintings, often by
artists who were forgotten or neglected, until his cottage in Cwm Rheidol
became a private gallery, the walls of every room hung closely with paintings, many of which had needed extensive restoration after years of neglect.

'No Welsh Art' is a showcase for some of the finest paintings in Peter Lord's collection, supplemented by paintings from the National Library's own extensive holdings. Here I must declare an interest because, as editor of *Planet*, I commissioned a number of Peter Lord's early essays on art, as well as one of his first books, *Words with Pictures* (Planet, 1995). For over three decades, therefore, I have followed his career as a collector and, in book after book, his emergence as the foremost historian of Welsh art.

The exhibition, as the ironic title implies, has a didactic purpose, expressed in the way paintings and other artefacts are displayed. As you enter the Library's spacious Gregynog Gallery, the visitor is guided to the left, past a portrait (a very good one, as it happens) of the unfortunate Llewelyn Wyn Griffith by Kyffin Williams, leading to themed sections: on patronage by the gentry, and increasingly in the nineteenth century, by the middle class; 'the visual world of the common people'; 'home-made art'; 'critics and historians'; 'painters and sculptors'; and 'Welsh identities' which range from how the English perceived us (as a joke mostly, or romantically displayed in magnificent landscapes), to expressions of Welsh history, myth and legend, religion, industry, and protest.

One of the most significant sections is devoted to the artisan painters of the nineteenth century. An emergent middle class, with income to spare, increasingly wished to see itself reflected in portraiture, no doubt as an echo of the gentry. The towns of Wales were usually too small to sustain resident artists, however, so a generation of artisan painters emerged who travelled the length and breadth of the country, often advertising their services in the local press. These were for the most part self-taught, or learned their technique from other artisan painters. As a result, their art can easily be dismissed as naïve, if judged by the high art aesthetic of metropolitan critics.

Peter Lord has long argued that a different approach is needed if we are to appreciate what these journeyman painters achieved. Take Hugh Hughes' painting, 'A Mother and Her Two Daughters' (1848), for example. The group is subtly arranged so that the mother's left hand gently holds the forearm of her younger daughter, while the pale curve of her arm sweeps up to her exposed shoulder and face, which is turned to engage with her older daughter standing to her left. There is a gentle, lingering contact between the three; it is a portrait of family intimacy, highlighted by the sombre undifferentiated background. Yet there is a certain stiffness to the group, almost as if the painting were a still life. It could easily be criticised by the aesthetic governing metropolitan portraiture.

Hugh Hughes, 'A Mother and Her Two Daughters' (1848). Peter Lord Collection.

The painting is in fact, however, a home-grown version of what Americans call folk art, which in the United States evolved its own aesthetic. As a result, work by artists such as Edward Hicks (1780–1849), John Brewster Jr (1766–1854), and Erastus Salisbury (1805–1900), is understood and highly prized, whereas in Wales – always looking over our shoulder towards

London – painters who were their contemporaries, such as Hugh Hughes (1790–1863), William Roos (1808–1878), and John Roberts (c1816–c1871) had been for the most part disregarded, until Peter Lord dug deep into the archives to recover what could be known about their lives, while at the same time assiduously collecting and restoring paintings, many of which had been ignored for generations.

Some at least of these artisan painters were aware of trends in London, however, and at times attempted to reproduce them, as in William Roos' 'Woman in a Blue Dress' (1839), the portrait of an elegant and affluent young woman who, the explanatory caption suggests, may have been a member of the London Welsh.

At times, too, artisan painters attempted landscapes on the grand Romantic scale. In the exhibition, this is represented by Hugh Hughes' 'Bwlch Llanberis' (1847), the largest canvas on display and the product of a commission. The canvas is divided by a huge V of sky which dominates the picture at the top, while at the same time accentuating the vertiginous downward thrust of the rocky slopes either side of the pass. It takes the viewer a while to reach the human focus of the scene at the base, where a horse and carriage labours upwards, preceded by a diminutive figure on foot, with another, a woman, before it, while a dog chases four sheep over a low stone parapet. Hugh Hughes had problems with perspective, and the road, as it winds to the left, is too wide. The power of the painting, however, is in the small group of humans, hardly noticed by the viewer at first but who, once seen, become the focus of attention.

This is landscape in the manner of high art, enfolded, as it were, within the artisan tradition in which Hugh Hughes operated, producing portraits on commission for the middle class. As the demand for portraiture began to wane, Hughes turned more to landscapes, and 'Bwlch Llanberis' must have been a lucrative commission for him.

It is interesting to compare it with other, later, landscapes, most notably, for me, Kyffin Williams' 'Llyn-y-Cau, Cadair Idris'. Here the eye is led from a pale sky at top left, to a grey-brown flank of the mountain which deepens at the centre to an impenetrable black echoed in the inky llyn below. If, in Hugh Hughes' landscape, humans are dwarfed by the sheer scale of the rocky walls of the pass, in this much smaller painting they are denied any presence at all. Nature is hostile, off limits.

Kyffin Williams, 'Llyn-y-Cau, Cadair Idris' (c1950). The National Library of Wales collection.

One painting in the exhibition has always intrigued me. It is 'Marquis of Anglesey' by John Roberts, Hen Walia, Caernarfon (not to be confused with the more well-known John Roberts, Llanystumdwy, mentioned above). Roberts was sixteen when he painted what is a fascinating example of a descending cultural model. The painting looks very much like an inn sign, and the likelihood is that Roberts drew on just such a sign above a pub that existed in Hen Walia at this time. The sign itself, however, was copied from a popular London aquatint by R Cooper and J Fuller, which in turn was based on a painting by Peter Stroehling, now in the Royal Collection. The Marquis was one of the heroes of the Battle of Waterloo, who famously had his leg shot from under him while consulting with Wellington. This image shows him leading the charge of the heavy brigade which, by this circuitous route, reached the young John Roberts in Caernarfon who would certainly never have seen the original, and probably not the aquatint – the inn sign, and John Roberts' rendition of it, being an echo of major events on the far away Continent, transfigured through art into an expression of British patriotic feeling. As such, it is also an expression of the ways in which many Welsh people identified with the English imperial project, buying into the 'British' state, which always meant England with contributions from its Celtic outliers.

John Roberts, Hen Walia, Caernarfon, 'Marquis of Anglesey' (1832). Peter Lord Collection.

Political/cultural issues aside, however, 'Marquis of Anglesey' is a fine example of folk art in American terms. The original by Stroehling is a good piece of military portraiture but of a kind that adorned the walls of numerous country seats in the eighteenth and nineteenth centuries. John Roberts' version, by contrast, is technically crude, yet it is the more striking with its vivid colours, the almost toy soldier face of the Marquis and his woodenly stepping charger. You could pass under Stroehling's painting in a mansion with barely a glance, but Roberts' version holds the eye. Who would not like to have it hanging on their wall?

This interplay between English perceptions of the Welsh and how we saw ourselves has complicating eddies. One concerns the figure of 'Poor Taff' which has its origin in English satirical prints of the late eighteenth century, several examples of which are displayed in the exhibition. The one which catches the eye, though, is an inn sign probably from the borders. 'Poor Taff' is portrayed here with a red nose and a downtrodden, pathetic gaze. He has a leek for a cockade and another leek for a sword with a dried herring strapped above it. He is kitted out with exaggeratedly wide riding boots and diminutive spurs. Taff presumably thinks he is dressed up as something of a swell, but instead of a horse, he is riding a goat, whose acrid stink would have blended with the herring and leeks to warn anyone off at his approach. Taff is an absurd, pathetic figure. The prints which this inn sign is based on were published in London for the diversion of the English and, despite being taken up by some Welsh people at the time, were an expression of the widespread prejudice in England against Wales and all things Welsh.

In the exhibition, the image of Poor Taff is challenged by another inn sign. This one comes from Hanner-y-Ffordd Inn in the Conwy valley and was painted around 1835 by an unknown artist. When it was acquired by Peter Lord, it was so covered with grime that the image could hardly be made out. When cleaned, however, a brilliant defiance of English perceptions was revealed; for though it is based on the Poor Taff iconography, it is a very different 'Taff' indeed who is on display here. The 'H Davies' on the sign is presumably the landlord who commissioned it. 'Taff' is no wimp, but a burly man, well dressed, with a feather cockade, not a leek, in his hat and good sharp spurs at his heels. He knows where he is going, knows what he wants, and is going to get it. This is indicated by the sign's motto, which plays on the patriotic 'Cymru am Byth'. The painter, no doubt under the direction of Mr H Davies, has converted this to '*Cymro* am Byth'. There would be no place for Poor Taffs in his pub, nor for the sneering English either.

(L) Anon, 'Inn Sign, Welsh Borders' (c1770–1820). Peter Lord Collection.
(R) Unknown artist, 'Sign of the Hanner-y-Ffordd Inn, Conwy Valley' (c1835).
Peter Lord Collection.

It is impossible to cover every aspect of such a wide-ranging exhibition, but after the display of artisan paintings, the most memorable section for me is devoted to the industrial painters of the early decades of the twentieth century. This is dominated by a powerful triptych in which Evans Walters' 'Bydd Myrdd o Ryfeddodau / Welsh Funeral Hymn' (1926) is flanked on either side by Archie Rhys Griffiths' 'On the Coal Tips' (c1929–31), and Maurice Sochachewsky's 'Their Burden' (1937).

In Griffiths' painting three women are returning from the tips with heavy sacks of hard-gathered coal; they are bending forward under the weight, their dresses are dull brown or grey, the only colour coming from the red shawl of the third woman. They are not talking to each other; behind them are the tips, and a grey-white sky of clouds, and far below the row on row of diminutive miners' cottages. There is something primeval about the women, something classical, as if they were part of a Greek tragic chorus or a manifestation of the Erinyes, the spirits of revenge, because these women are indomitable, unconquerable.

Maurice Sochachewsky's 'Their Burden', painted when he was nineteen and a visitor to the Valleys, has a similar sense of defiance in adversity. Here a husband and wife are descending from the tips carrying a sack of scavenged coal across their shoulders. They are poorly dressed and the man looks grim, his eyes cast down and to his left. The woman, however, stares defiantly straight at the viewer, the brilliant whites of her eyes giving them a compelling intensity, filled with you cannot quite say what – hate, perhaps, or challenge, or the edge of misery? Her eyes dominate the picture and follow the viewer around; they will not release you. It takes a while to realise that 'Their Burden' is also an expression of love. The woman's right hand reaches across to support her husband's shoulder, as if giving him her strength under the burden of the sack; while his left hand is wrapped protectively around her left shoulder. Times are desperate, but love holds them together. It is a profound image for a nineteen-year-old to have painted.

Evan Walters, 'Bydd Myrdd o Ryfeddodau / Welsh Funeral Hymn' (1926).
The National Library of Wales collection.

The centrepiece of the triptych is more disturbing and perhaps not entirely in ways intended by Evan Walters. Four naked boys are displayed on what might be a black tip. Each has the stigmata, bloody and raw. Far above them is a congregation of the religious, dressed in black, with a black chapel behind them. As the caption to the painting explains, the hymn in question is 'Bydd Myrdd o Ryfeddau' (There Will Be Myriad Wonders) which celebrates the soul, freed at death from suffering on Earth – suffering which has to be endured while we are here below. The painting is a bitter protest against such resignation. The crucified boys are victims of a ruthless industrialism which exploited and destroyed them. It should be opposed, not watched impassively by the congregation on the black hill above.

Yet I found it disturbing in another way. The delicate pallor of the boys' skin is highlighted by the blackness of the coal they are lying on. The boys are clearly on the verge of pubescence, their genitals discreetly covered, and I find it impossible not to see a highly charged erotic element here. Almost certainly Evan Walters did not intend this, and perhaps my response is a reflection of different times and perceptions. For me, it made 'Bydd Myrdd o Ryfeddodau / Welsh Funeral Hymn' an uncomfortable painting, compared with those by Archie Rhys Griffiths and Maurice Sochachewsky.

The juxtaposition of these paintings is at once a protest against poverty and injustice and, in the case of 'On the Coal Tips' and 'Their Burden', a celebration of human endurance and the will to live. They are defiant, and in their way, triumphant.

They are, of course, political, as are other paintings in the exhibition, none more so than Peter Davies' 'Tŷ Haf' (1984) In it, an English second home is burning fiercely, the canvas dominated by heavily impasto'd orange and yellow flames. There is a suggestion of a lake or reservoir at bottom left (a hint at Tryweryn?), while at bottom right a small printed Union Jack has been glued to the paint – the British flag, and all it stands for, doesn't belong here, it is stuck on, an intrusion and an outrage. In the brochure that accompanies the exhibition, 'Tŷ Haf' is given prominence with a full page to itself, bled to the edges. Its vibrant and dynamic colours reinforce the message of the painting which, itself, is quite small.

Beca (Peter Davies), 'Tŷ Haf' (1984). Peter Lord Collection.

As I said at the beginning, the exhibition has a didactic purpose: to decolonise Welsh painting, and to locate it within the traditions of our culture and society. This, of course, is what Peter Lord has been doing in book after book for several decades, and in this sense the exhibition is the visual culmination of his life's work.

For the visitor, other questions may arise that are not answered because they are not within the remit of the exhibition. One is the relationship of

Welsh art to the European tradition, because no nation's art exists in isolation. Portrait and landscape painting, for example, reflects trends and styles that are part of a common European artistic heritage.

Another is aesthetic. All the paintings on display reflect Wales in one way or another, but viewed from a painterly perspective they are not all equally good as works of art. This is of course a contentious issue and involves a degree of subjectivity. Moreover, value judgement depends on the aesthetics of the tradition within which a painter is working. The aesthetics of French Impressionism, for example, cannot be applied to the great tradition of Australian Aborigine bark painting which operates on a very different understanding of the nature and purpose of art. By the same token, Welsh artisan painting of the nineteenth century needs to be understood in its own terms, aesthetic as well as social, before individual paintings can be evaluated. At this exhibition, it is left to the viewer.

Where do we go from here? Come September this year, the exhibition will close. The paintings belonging to the National Library will go back into storage. As to Peter Lord's extraordinary collection, the future is very uncertain. It would form the invaluable nucleus of a national gallery, but of course we do not have our own. For years, Peter Lord has sought a home for the collection, perhaps as a permanent display within an existing gallery. Several possibilities have seemed, at one time or another, promising, but they have all broken down, usually on the issue of financing. The collection is no longer housed in the cottage in Cwm Rheidol, and so when the exhibition closes, it is a question as to whether the paintings, drawings, and numerous artefacts, can somehow be stored. If they can't, then it is possible that it will be sold and dispersed at auction. This would be a national disaster, because, no matter how deep your pockets are, this collection could never be re-assembled.

Scotland has its national gallery, Ireland has its national gallery, but Wales has none. The argument that we lack a sufficiently rich and varied artistic tradition to justify one is refuted by this exhibition. The argument that as a nation we are too poor to afford one is merely pathetic. The small

Danish island of Bornholm in the Baltic is dependent on agriculture and tourism, so not unlike the greater part of Wales. It also happens to have a special quality of light which has attracted painters to the island for the past 150 years. As a result, there is a distinct school of painters associated with the island. Bornholmers are proud of this tradition and celebrate it in a purpose-built modern gallery, Bornholms Kunstmuseum. It is not, as might be expected, situated in the island's principal town, Rønne, but by itself along the coast. The Kunstmuseum is light and airy, the paintings superbly displayed, and when I visited a few years ago, it was thronged with visitors, both Bornholmers, and outsiders like myself.

The question is: why does Wales not have such a gallery? Even Guyana, one of the poorest nations in the Caribbean, has a national art gallery in Georgetown because it is proud of its art. It is true that the National Museum in Cardiff displays Welsh art but it does not see this as its primary purpose. It is true that the rich and varied tradition of our art has only recently been appreciated. It is also true that certain painters have achieved national recognition. Kyffin Williams is one, Ceri Richards another. What we have not done is achieve a critical mass of interest among the populace, sufficient to demand an independent national gallery, or even to care about the fate of our art.

A depressing example of this is what has happened to Mildred Eldridge's extraordinary mural, 'The Dance of Life' (1953). This was commissioned to decorate the refectory of the hospital in Gobowen, where it was displayed for many years until it was relocated to Wrexham University. More recently, it has been relocated yet again, this time to a private school near Ellesmere. A major work of Welsh art is not only in private hands, it is in private hands in England and unavailable to the Welsh public. How did this happen? Who allowed it to happen? Nobody is providing an explanation.

It is an extraordinary state of affairs. In a national gallery, 'The Dance of Life' would have a significant place – even a room of its own; yet we have let this national treasure slip through our fingers, and why? Because we do not care.

Everyone who can should try to get to the National Library to see '*Dim Celf Gymreig*' / '*No Welsh Art*' because there has never been an exhibition like it, and unless our attitude to the achievement of Welsh art changes, there may never be another. The exhibition points the way: we need a national gallery, and we need it *now*.

John Barnie, a former editor and publisher of *Planet* magazine and book imprint, is a prize-winning writer, editor and critic. His latest publication, a broadside in a new series from Rack Press, *Kaleidoscope: Images from a Disordered World*, was issued in October 2024.

SHAPESHIFTING

ANGHARAD PENRHYN JONES EXPLORES SEVEN RECENT BOOKS
THAT DELINEATE AND CELEBRATE WOMEN'S LIVES, IN ALL THEIR
WAXING, WANING PHASES

Quotations from Welsh-language books translated by Angharad Penrhyn Jones

I'M WRITING THIS PIECE ON A MISTY MORNING ON ONE OF THOSE limbo days between Christmas and the New Year. It's been a strange, disorientating time, and the weather feels fitting. I spent Christmas day alone, my eighteen-year-old daughter having flown the nest to go travelling, my parents having recently emigrated. I could have joined my parents but, practical issues aside, perhaps felt the need to sit in the fog for a while, to allow myself to experience this loss of bearings. My newfound freedom feels both wonderful and daunting: almost as wonderful and daunting as holding a newborn baby in my arms in 2006, asking myself how on earth I was going to deal with this new life – and feeling my old one melt away like snow. To be a woman is often to re-imagine and re-shape ourselves over and over. This past year I've read books by women who've made me feel less alone as I face the proverbial empty nest, perimenopause, and a career stalled by single parenting; women whose experiences mirror mine; women at different life stages writing about their relationships with themselves and others, within the walls of patriarchy.

As a white woman, of course, it is all too easy for me to ignore the ways in which white supremacy affords me privilege whilst oppressing many of my fellow sisters. In her important book, *Why I'm No Longer Talking to White People about Race* (Bloomsbury Publishing, 2017), Reni Eddo-Lodge refers to this 'invisible whiteness' and the blissful lack of awareness with which we move through the world:

> I write – and read – to assure myself that other people have felt what I'm feeling too, that it isn't just me, that this is real, and valid, and true. I am only acutely aware of race because I've been rigorously marked out as different by the world I know for as long as I can remember. Although I analyse invisible whiteness and ponder its exclusionary nature often, I watch as an outsider. I understand that this isn't the case for most white people, who move through the world blissfully unaware of their own race until its dominance is called into question. [...] To be white is to be human; to be white is universal. I only know this because I am not.

These words came to mind as I read *Oedolyn(ish!)* [Adult(ish)] (Lolfa, 2024), a memoir by twenty-nine year-old comedian and broadcaster, Melanie Owen. She brings Eddo-Lodge's point home in an entertaining and moving account of the lessons life has taught her so far. Describing herself, in her self-deprecating tone, as 'merch fach Frown o gefn gwlad Ceredigion' [a little Brown girl from rural Ceredigion], she tells us plainly that growing up as a Brown child in Aberystwyth had its 'disadvantages'. Her book, loose and conversational in style, covers a range of experiences which will feel familiar to many women, of all ages: from imposter syndrome, to the loss of a precious friendship, to the challenges of dating. While she could resent having also to take on the labour of educating the white reader about structural racism, she does so with humour and an impressively light touch.

I learned about the phenomenon of 'adultification' in relation to Black girls, how they tend to physically develop earlier than white girls, especially those of Caribbean origin, becoming taller and stronger before their white counterparts. These girls are often treated like adults, and sexualised, when they are still children. I also learned that Black girls perform best in schools, academically, but are also the demographic most likely to be kicked out for bad behaviour. Adultification means that Black girls are treated more harshly than white girls, a phenomenon which also plays out in a court of law: black girls are more likely to go to a juvenile detention centre or to jail, where a white girl might receive a warning or community service for the same crime. Melanie Owen, drawing on academic studies, writes about how this discrimination affected her as a young woman, particularly in terms of her relationship with her body:

> Achos fod 'na gyn lleied o ferched Du eraill yn yr ardal i fi gael uniaethu gyda nhw, doeddwn i ddim yn siŵr pam o'n i'n cael fy nhrin yn fwy llym, neu pham nad oeddwn i'n cael fy niogelu yn yr un ffordd â'r merched eraill.... [translation follows]

> Because there were so few Black women in my area who I could relate to, I wasn't sure why I was being treated more harshly, or why I wasn't being protected in the same way as other girls. But I knew I was different. When I looked in the mirror, trying to understand what made me different, my naïve eyes didn't see my colour or my race. The realisation that racist discrimination would play a part in my life hadn't yet sprouted in my childish mind. But I did see a difference in terms of how fat I felt. I looked in the mirror and saw how wide I was, how round my belly and jiggly my legs. This, I decided, was the reason I was treated as though I were of less value.

The description of her subsequent descent into bulimia is frightening, and she admits that, although she no longer induces herself to vomit, she does not remember the last time she was able to eat a meal without experiencing guilt. Reading her story, we see how politics is so very, very personal, as the seventies feminists had it. Politics – in the broadest sense of how society organises itself, who has the power and who is acted upon, who is the 'universal' subject and who is the object – penetrates every aspect of our lives, our bodies.

Melanie Owen's debut book is a breath of fresh air in the shockingly white scene of Welsh publishing, and it is also subversive in its treatment of Cymraeg: she writes as she speaks, peppering the page with English phrases and words and a mish-mash of dialects, refusing to modify her voice to conform to the norms of 'proper' standardised Welsh. 'Os ydi fy nghymysgedd o dafodieithoedd gwahanol yn weindo chi lan, rhowch y teledu mlaen, gwyliwch y newyddion ac mi welwch chi'r pethau gwir uffernol sy'n digwydd yn y byd.' [If my mix of different dialects winds you up, switch on the TV, watch the news, and you'll see the truly terrible things that are happening in the world.] She uses footnotes throughout to make amusing asides. Her voice is singularly hers; it is both vulnerable and extremely funny. To try to recount her jokes and her perfect punch-lines would do her a grave injustice, but *Oedolyn-ish* made me laugh out loud often and almost choke on my food. It also made me well up, cringe so hard I wanted the ground to swallow me up (her anecdote about the croissant will haunt me for the rest of my days), and feel the fire of injustice in my belly.

Despite being almost twenty years older than Owen, I found her a wise companion, and wished I'd learned some of those hard lessons myself, earlier in life. She unpacks the meaning of 'love bombing' and 'gaslighting' and 'anxious attachment', for example: concepts I wish I'd understood as a younger woman, even if they have the ring of self-help cliché by now. It's a book I'll be lending my daughter on her return from her travels. Melanie states that she feels protective of women younger than herself, 'as if I were turning every young woman into the younger sister I never had.' Moreover, I was interested to see, in the acknowledgments, that the book wouldn't have existed without two mentors: the hugely accomplished writers Bethan Gwanas and Marged Tudur. To see women in publishing quietly offering a leg up to the next generation is, in itself, hopeful.

Two other recent titles also celebrate how women have worked together in Wales, in this case to challenge the political status quo: *Merched Peryglus* [Dangerous Women] (Honno, 2023) and *Gwir Gofnod o Gyfnod* [Setting the Record Straight] (Honno, 2024), the latter of which is published in separate language editions. These anthologies are partly accounts of oral history, *Gwir Gofnod* drawing on the work of Women's Archive Wales. They constitute an important record of the unglamorous and sometimes dangerous work undertaken by political representatives and activists to further certain causes. These include the Welsh language, autonomy for Wales, and the autonomy of women in a rural, patriarchal society where traditionally we have been excluded from the corridors of power. *Gwir Gofnod* and *Merched Peryglus* both include an impressive range of voices, and it's interesting to see the cross-referencing and overlapping between the different accounts: while it can feel a little repetitive at times, it's also apposite, for this is all about collaboration, a community of women, rather than individuals with discrete stories. These women have stood on the shoulders of other women – sometimes literally, when taking direct action. S4C, the Welsh Language channel, wouldn't exist, for example, had it not been for the courage of female activists who protested against the UK Government's U-turn by climbing television masts, as is documented so vividly in *Merched Peryglus*. Younger women drew on the experiences of older campaigners; they sat in police cells and prison cells together, singing songs passed down by their mothers and grandmothers. The metaphor that came to mind whilst reading these anthologies about Welsh trailblazers was that of a patchwork quilt, with its symmetries and echoing patterns: a form of art, of course, traditionally practised by women.

The image of the patchwork quilt, as it happens, is used to powerful effect in a play by Sharon Morgan, the first in a trilogy about three different phases of a girl and woman's life: *Dramâu'r Rhosys Cochion* [plays produced by the Rhosys Cochion drama company] (Honno, 2024). 'Ede Hud' [Magic Thread] is a portrait of girlhood, located in the coal valley of Dyffryn Aman; 'Holl Liwiau'r Enfys' [All the Colours of the Rainbow] portrays the sexual and political awakening of a young woman in the village of Llandyfaelog in Sir Gaerfyrddin; while 'Trafaelu ar y Trên Glas' [Travelling on the Blue Train], located in Cardiff, examines the impacts of menopause, ageing and grief. The first play names the female relatives in a girl's life – the 'insignificant' women with their 'unimportant' stories; women who, in fact, have spun their own magical worlds within this world, created their own private spheres, used alchemy to create dynamite in kitchen pans. The girl sleeps under a patchwork quilt:

A odd y ferch fach yn cysgu mewn gwely mowr plu dan y cwilt nath mam mam ei mam o ffrogie'i modrybedd a trwseri ei ewythrod. A odd y ferch fach yn cysgu ym mywyde ei pherthnase.

And the little girl slept in a big feather bed under the quilt her mother's mother's mother made from her aunt's dresses and her uncle's trousers. And the little girl slept amid her relatives' lives.

Sharon Morgan's words are tricky to translate since they're written in the dialect of Sir Gâr. The actor and playwright, like Melanie Owen, rejects the formal, standardised Cymraeg, and revels in the language of her tribe and community, a language that feels intimate and domestic (the volume includes a glossary, to help readers from other parts of the country). These plays, written between 1996 and 2008, feel radical in terms of content and form. There is no plot or character development or conventional dialogue, no single authoritative Narrator, and the monologues read like free-verse poetry at times, occasionally falling into rhyme. They are circular, impressionistic, dream-like, containing lines from fairy tale, popular songs and hymns. There is an incantatory feeling to the text, and the effect is cumulative. By the time I'd reached the end of the third play, where we witness the death of the mother figure, I felt overtaken by emotion. We have been with the girl in her grandmother's garden as she picks flowers for her mother; now the child is singing a lullaby to her dying Mami, her identity obliterated as she lets her go, the way a mother has to let her child leave the nest:

Wi'n neb nawr,
wi'n ddalen lân,
Sai'n gwbod o le des i
na pwy wdw' i

I'm nobody now,
I'm a clean page,
I don't know where I came from
or who I am.

In her introduction, Sharon Morgan refers to the use of Narrator, Witness
and Event; the relationship between these three levels is fluid. The
Witnesses have been situated outdoors, and specifically in gardens: they
are not confined by walls. These gardens have mythical resonances. Morgan
writes about the 'importance of the garden as a feminine space transferred
from generation to generation, a symbol of personal creativity, where a
woman can express that which can't be expressed elsewhere.' In the third
play, we read about a woman engaged in an act of burial: 'Mae'n claddu'r
gwirionedd yng ngwaelod yr ardd, yn ddwfwn ddwfwn yn y ddaear ddu'
(poetry nerds: this second clause is an example of cynghanedd) [she buries
the truth at the bottom of the garden, deep, deep in the black earth'].
Women's stories have been buried since the beginning of time, and it takes
courage to unearth them in a society which dismisses our truths. Morgan,
herself a single mother, is unashamedly political in her agenda as a playwright, arguing that Welsh-speaking women are doubly oppressed; the
young woman in the second play experiences a political awakening after
meeting a new friend, Siân, and starts marching for her country and language. 'Welsh women have always lived within double shackles', Morgan
writes, 'by being part of a small nation ruled by a more powerful nation,
and by living under patriarchy's thumb.'

This quest for freedom is an important thread running through the three
plays, and it is conveyed through striking imagery. There are references to
running up mountains and pulling off clothes, rushing down rapids, sailing
across seas in a boat made of leaves, rising up into the clouds like a lark,
rising above the village and reaching the moon. In a nod to Virginia Woolf,
the young woman in 'Holl Liwiau'r Enfys' creates a secret space in her own
room: here, she can be free:

Mae'n danso'n ei stafell,
gall neb arall ddod miwn
Mae'n breifat mae'n glyd
Mae'n saff yn 'i stafell
Hi bia'r stafell

Gall neb arall ddod miwn
Ma' lle a ma' amser
Hi bia'r byd
Gall neb arall ddod miwn 'ma
Hi bia fe gyd.

She dances in her room,
no one else can come in
It's private it's cosy
It's safe in her room
She owns the room

No one else can come in
There's space and there's time
She owns the world
No one else can come in here
She owns all of it.

And at the end of this play, the young woman packs her suitcase, ready
to embark on an adventure: a passage that moved me deeply having
watched my own daughter pack her rucksack before setting off on the
train from Machynlleth to East Africa, her heart in her throat. This
young woman from Llandyfaelog packs 'a lot of new clothes and hope
and longing and fear and excitement and the river's clean water and
flowers from the hedge...':

A mae'n barod.
'Oh girls, look at the sky.'
Mae'n mynd wrth ei hunan
yn betrus yn syfrdan
i dorri ei llwybr
ar Fynydd Breuddwydion.

And she's ready.
'Oh girls, look at the sky.'
She goes alone
in fear in wonder
to cut her path
on the Mountain of Dreams.

When the older woman in 'Travelling on the Blue Train' reaches menopause, however, she mourns her loss of identity as she stops menstruating;
she is on a train to a different kind of destination.

Ma' hiraeth arno'i am ga'l bod yn sownd i'r lliad
a cownto'r dyddie yn 'y nghorff
a timlo rythme'r tonne yn 'y ngwa'd
[...]
Sdim tonne'n torri ar 'y nrha'th
Wi'n llonydd a wi'n rhydd
Ond mae'n hen rhyddid od
Pwy wdw' i nawr
A le fi fod?

I'm longing to be stuck to the moon
Counting the days in my body
Feeling the waves' rhythms in my blood
[...]

No waves are breaking on my beach
I'm still and I'm free
But it's a strange old freedom
Who am I now
And where am I meant to be?

While these plays confront the dark side of women's lives – a woman dies on the side of a road after giving birth; an old auntie screams as she remembers an event she cannot talk about; girls are groomed by society to be 'good' rather than happy – there is also a playful and joyous spirit at work here. The wildness of the natural world, friendships with other women, exploration and song and dance: these offer a form of salvation even within the shadow of the high walls. And there are flowers, everywhere.

From the valleys of rural Wales to the urban sprawl of Los Angeles, Miranda July's novel, *All Fours* (Canongate, 2024) is also preoccupied with the question of what happens to a woman when she reaches mid-life. I believe this wry and devastatingly astute novel will push some women, and perhaps men, to change their lives. It examines desire and creative freedom and bodily trauma; it asks us to reflect on what it might mean for a married woman and mother to hide away in a room of her own and engage in a dangerous liaison with a younger man from a car rental business. The protagonist remains unnamed: the reader can step into her shoes, fill in the blanks. An artist of some kind (as vague as their name), this forty-five-year-old 'minor celebrity' sets off on a road trip to New York but ends up creating, in a motel close to home, a hyper-feminine space: luxurious, sensual; private as the womb, and leading to its own kind of rebirth. The novel subverts the stereotypically masculine trope of the road trip; the scenes in the womb-room are visceral, as the character embarks on an epic psychological journey and a reckoning with herself. *All Fours* also subverts the 'coming of age' story: this woman is coming, so to speak, into middle age. The writing about masturbation and sex (straight, as well as lesbian) is eye-wateringly bawdy, sexy, and at times hilarious; and I was touched by the portrayal of the platonic love between female friends, who speak with such wit and tenderness about the taboo subjects often ignored in literature. It is true that July's bisexual female protagonist, drawing as she does on huge material privilege, can afford to give a great deal of thought to questions of personal liberation and mid-life fulfilment. Yet *All Fours* also illuminates the ways in which friendship can be a literal lifeline. No woman, is turns out, is an island. And while there is something solipsistic about the lens, we are encouraged to question the institute of marriage and the nuclear family, to think about how these institutions might be re-mapped. In this respect, it's a subversive piece of work.

In an interview on *The Daily Show* (15 May, 2024), Miranda July, a performing artist and film-maker as well as writer (who might herself be described as a minor celebrity) explained that she wrote the book that she would have wanted to read when she turned forty – perhaps to know that her experiences are 'real, and valid, and true', to echo Reni Eddo-Lodge. She pointed out that love songs are often about desire in those teenage years when hormones go haywire. But what happens when a woman reaches a cliff-edge in terms of her own hormone levels (and the cover of her book displays a cliff bathed in golden light, an image both daunting and beautiful): where's the story about this change, this metamorphosis? Where are the love stories? 'We're about to fall off a cliff,' cries the narrator to her friend Jordi. 'We're going to be totally different people in a few years.' 'We should be allowed one year during perimenopause to be free, knowing the end is coming,' proclaims the narrator's friend, Mary. 'It's such a dangerous time, right before the window closes.' The narrator's own story happens when she disappears into a room, goes off the radar, is driven to reinvent herself:

> I tried to remember how Pinocchio had become a real boy. It had something to do with being in a whale, maybe saving his father's life. I hadn't done anything like that. But surely a woman was more complex than a puppet boy and she might become herself not once-and-for-all, but cyclically: waxing, waning, sometimes disappearing altogether.

The novel includes a visual aid to help explain what happens to oestrogen levels in perimenopause, along with a detailed conversation between the protagonist and a gynaecologist about the physical changes that happen as she falls off the 'oestrogen cliff' ('sudden bloodbaths, ghost cycles with cramps but no bleeding, thick black blood eels'): we are in the room with them as the narrator undergoes a vaginal examination. At the waiting clinic, she observes that the different generations of women waiting alongside her should each have their own space, separated by a fish tank: 'maybe three rooms/two tanks through which we could peer wordlessly at one another, knowing each age was an evaporating dream we'd either had or would eventually have and there was no way to penetrate each other's sphere.' *All Fours* is partly an attempt to pin down the 'evaporating dream', to hold on to the thread that connects generations of women, to pass on knowledge and courage, to refuse to be divided by a society which would rather we stay silent on embarrassing bodily topics, and internalise feelings of shame.

We read text exchanges between the protagonist and her friends about the positive and negative aspects of menopause: at times this feels less like fiction and more like the author's personal investigation into a transition she's living through; either way, I found this section insightful, informative and at times incredibly amusing. It's also sobering: the protagonist's grandmother and aunt died by suicide in mid-life, and the book's acknowledgements suggest that July has been affected here by personal experience. There is an association between menopause and suicide ideation. *All Fours* reminds us that medical misogyny is one of the challenges of our age.

Miranda July, like her protagonist, experienced Foetal Maternal Haemorrhage on giving birth, and subsequent trauma: this, too, is a recurring theme in the book, along with detail of PTSD flashbacks and a sense that the narrator has been abandoned by the medical establishment to deal with these horrors alone. 'In patriarchy, your body is technically not your own until you pass the reproductive age,' says the gynaecologist offhandedly in the clinic – and yet patriarchy is not interested in the fallout from reproduction either, leaving women to form online support groups after giving birth to stillborn babies, where often all they can write is: 'WTF'? There are so many questions, and no answers.

It's important to note here that July does not reduce womanhood to simplistic, essentialist, notions of biology: she does not present gender as a binary; her child (both in the novel and in her actual life) is referred to as they/them; her narrator acknowledges that trans people face their own challenges. Still, her own story, and fears about ageing, matter:

> If birth was being thrown energetically up into the air, we aged as we rose. At the height of our ascent we were middle-aged and then we fell for the rest of our lives, the whole second half. Falling might take just as long, but it was nothing like rising. The whole time you were rising you could not imagine what came next in your particular, unique journey; you could not see around the corner. Whereas falling ended the same way for everyone. [...] Trans men, women, and less gendered people were another story (always), but if my hetero tale mattered (and suddenly it seemed like it did) then this was a very abrupt conclusion. I had not seen this coming and so I had not lived my life accordingly. [...] I had sat on my nest like a complacent hen, certain that when I felt like strutting about again everything would be exactly as it was before. [...] Without knowing it, without really understanding it, I had been a body for other people but I had not gotten to have one myself.

There is a striking parallel between *All Fours* and Sharon Morgan's trilogy with the emphasis on dance as providing an almost transcendental experience, a way of breaking out of Time itself. In July's world, as in Morgan's, dance offers a kind of spiritual as well as a sensual freedom. Through dance, we can find our way back into our bodies, back into our true selves – as subjects, not objects, capable of feeling genuine joy despite everything: perhaps the most radical act of all.

In the Welsh feminist press Honno's anthology, about what it means to be a woman in the twenty-first century, *Hi–Hon* [She–Her], Mabli Siriol Jones, director of the Social Change Lab and former chair of the Welsh

Language Society, cautions women against falling into the trap of victimhood. This is a wide-ranging, engaging volume, in which ten women offer their perspectives in the form of short stories, essays and illustrations. Jones' essay feels more conventional and traditionally 'masculine' than the other pieces, its structure linear: it's the least formally creative piece in the book. But it's a thoughtful and important contribution. Having discussed the harrowing case of Sarah Everard's murder in 2021 at the hands of a police officer, and the general discourse around male violence against women – along with the failure of the criminal justice system to tackle it – she raises uncomfortable points about the direction in which mainstream feminist politics is moving:

> This [feminist politics] focuses entirely on 'identity' [...] The missing link is an understanding of broader structures and the nature of power in our society, especially social class. It focuses on the ways individuals treat one another and how power moves between them, but does this without an analysis of structural forces, such as the power of capital and state [...]. It is an individualistic politics, rather than a collective one.

Jones warns us of the dangers of making fear, pain and trauma a core part of what it means to be a woman. Turning to feminist Wendy Brown's theory of 'wounded attachments', she claims that our attachment to suffering can lead to both a sense of moral superiority and helplessness, neither of which helps our cause. It can also makes us more likely to fall prey to reactionary forces who, for example, want to pit cisgender women against trans women. A feminism that defines itself according to specific bodily traumas and suffering becomes a feminism that insists on gatekeeping womanhood; it is one that will weaponise women's fears and persuade us that there are threats to our safety where none exists. 'It takes attention away from the real risks,' she argues, 'the cisgender men who are the main perpetrators of violence, and a state that does not provide support to victims.'

I would have liked to see an acknowledgment here of the importance of sharing stories and bearing witness to one another's traumatic experiences, which is known to be a crucial part of any recovery process. Jones assumes that we tell stories about our suffering in the hope that men will 'listen'; in truth, it's often about the need to have our suffering 'witnessed', to experience empathy, and to know that we are not alone. But Jones makes a very compelling argument against living in a state of suspicion towards others, at a time when trans women, in particular, face an increasing level of hatred and danger as they are vilified as the threatening 'other', scapegoated in vicious culture wars. She believes that to make progress as women we need to focus on our sense of agency and willpower within patriarchy: she herself refuses to give in to feelings of fear and fragility while walking alone in Cardiff at night. If women stay at home, she argues, we perpetuate the problem. Women around the globe living in oppressive systems find ways of resisting and being happy. 'We go out at night, make love, work, take chances and exercise our physical, sexual and mental freedom every day – despite the risks,' she writes. 'Even when we have experienced violence, life goes on and offers so much beyond trauma.' While she was writing her piece, one of the writer's friends was sexually assaulted. Jones started to question her own arguments, but ultimately stuck to her belief that as women we cannot live in fear and a state of victimhood. We have to join the movement to tackle the root causes of our oppression; we must all play our part in tackling the structural issues and demanding material change. We have to 're-imagine' everything, she writes – and who can disagree with that, with the importance of imagination and creativity in re-shaping ourselves, our world? And it's a world, she reminds us, that belongs to us all.

Books Discussed

Why I'm No Longer Talking To White People about Race, Reni Eddo-Lodge (Bloomsbury Publishing, 2017)

Oedolyn(ish!): Y Gwersi Dwi Wedi eu Dysgu Fel Nad Oes Rhaid i Chi Wneud, Melanie Owen (Lolfa, 2024)

Merched Peryglus, ed Angharad Tomos and TE Cathan Davies (Honno, 2024)

Gwir Gofnod o Gyfnod, ed Catrin Edwards and Kate Sullivan (Honno, 2024)

Dramâu'r Rhosys Cochion: Ede Hud, Lliwiau'r Enfys, Trafaelu ar y Trên Glas, Sharon Morgan (Honno, 2024)

All Fours, Miranda July (Canongate, 2024)

Hi–Hon, ed Catrin Beard and Esyllt Angharad Lewis (Honno, 2024)

Angharad Penrhyn Jones is a freelance writer, editor and bookseller based in Machynlleth. Her book about women activists, *Here We Stand: Women Changing the World* (Honno, 2014; Left Book Club, 2015), co-edited with Helena Earnshaw, won the Bread & Roses prize for Radical Publishing. Angharad participates in *Talwrn y Beirdd* on BBC Radio Cymru with the Llewod Cochion poetry team of Dinas Mawddwy. She writes regularly for literary magazine *O'r Pedwar Gwynt*, of which she was Associate Editor for three years. She has also produced and directed TV documentaries, for which she won BAFTA Wales awards.

FOREMOTHER:
ARMENIAN FAMILY MEMOIR

NANEH V HOVHANNISYAN

I'M ON A HUNT FOR A PHOTOGRAPH. IN THE HEAD-AND-SHOULDERS image I remember, I am a couple of years old, sitting between two maternal great-grandmothers, both with head scarves covering their foreheads which attest to their Ottoman heritage, their smiles softening their stern looks. The picture was taken in a studio in late 1970s Armenia. When I've found it, on its bottom right-hand side I will see the photographer's name on a logo. The atelier, as we called it, an extinct landmark of my childhood now, was on Yerevan's Kievyan փողոց: Kiev Street. Or should that be 'Kyiv' now?

I've a few weeks to find it before my operation, which involves general anaesthetic. As the day gets closer, I keep tidying the house, putting things in order just in case, rearranging drawers, sorting through the albums I'll be leaving to my daughter. Because if you're middle-aged, when there is induced deep sleep, there's always the risk of not waking.

In the image, to one side of me is my mother's paternal grandmother, whom I've heard lots about but don't remember. Great-grandmother Ashkhen (Ashkhen tati to us) is another story. Even without the aid of that photo, the only one of her we have, I can recall her in an instant: a petite figure clad in solid dark colours, dainty features, a pale complexion, and a kerchief – aylukh, as she said. The way she'd surreptitiously pull rubles out of her bra, count them, hand them over to me and my brother, instructing us to go to the shop for waffles or ice-cream or biscuits. Vapli, marozhni, pecheni:

these were new, Russian words for her, folded into her Armenian sentences. She had trouble pronouncing them uncorrupted.

– Gran, say 'passport'.

– Bashibort, I know that one.

We laughed, then asked her to say another.

– Eeh, get lost, she chuckled.

In fact, *did* she have trouble with those words, if she seemed happy to adjust them?

Hers was a frictionless, soft presence in our lives, free of discipline, judgement or exercise of power. We children adored her the way people adore their pets, without the complicated, contradictory feelings reserved for the merely human. We had a common bond; that is, both she and we were at a slight remove from the mainstream of life, not quite adults.

When tati came from Yerevan to stay with us, my brother and I helped her shower – she, sitting on a chair, and we, five and ten years old, lathering her back and legs and arms.

– How embarrassing, vuy, that's enough, darlings.

We lived in a dormitory room in an industrial town, waiting for state housing to materialise. She was a widow in her seventies, eager to see her first (favourite?) grandchild get a permanent home. Talking to my mother about an elderly acquaintance who had become a widower: I'd marry him, sweetheart, if I knew he'd leave you his house. A canny woman, my great-grandmother.

She could barely read, but in her handbag-sized address book were written, in hesitant hand, the phone numbers of long-time friends and extended family. Holding the receiver tightly, as though the strength of the line depended on the firmness of her grip, she would turn the dial six times and wait, her free hand playing with the wire. No glasses or hearing aids (were these available?) And when the person answered, Aha, Sirvard ջան? (that term of endearment, jan). Now both hands held the receiver. How's everyone? And so-and-so? Once she'd passed on her news, cheered up her interlocutor, and arranged a visit, she would hang up and bring her daughter, my grandmother Seda, up to speed: Svarik is a good lad. We chuckled. What, wrong again? Ooph, Slavik.

I am the eldest of Ashkhen's sixteen great-grandchildren, my mother the eldest of nine grandchildren, meaning I knew her the longest; also, having received more of her stories, I must hold more of them, too. What have I learnt from her? What will I take to the grave, should I not survive this operation? Which stories should I pass on to my daughter? For aren't stories received to be shared?

What do I share with her? After all, she's not just a face in a photograph but a voice in my head.

We know she was a child genocide escapee. In 1914, with her mother, Èva, six siblings, paternal uncles and others, she fled from her ancestral home in modern-day Turkey (then the Ottoman empire) to modern-day Armenia (then in the Russian Empire). She was five or six. She didn't know her birthday.

Did she have a birth certificate – in Ottoman Turkish, written in Perso-Arabic script? If so, I might be able to read it with my university Arabic. Or later, a bashibort in imperial Russian orthography? Or later still, one in reformed, Soviet, orthography – Armenian, or Russian? Did she sign documents with a thumbprint? Write her name in hesitant hand? Do we have nothing official to testify to her existence?

Thankfully, we do have her voice, fortuitously captured one 1980s evening on a reel-to-reel by my parents. They tell her to chat normally, as this interview is a practice run. She approves the idea of straightening things in advance of the real recording.

Of the seven siblings, only she would survive the journey: the railways, the gendarmes, famine and dehydration, then diseases. On the tape: We were in three-four carts, running away under machine gun fire. Ooh, there were lots like us. Each in one place, some died, some disappeared by the time we got here.

Here, in what must have been 1915 or '16, wasn't Armenia, officially, but 'Erivanskaya gubernia' (Erivan governorate in Russian). The Tsarist administrative unit encompassed the bulk of the present-day republic, known as Eastern Armenia or Russo–Armenia (Iranian, earlier), plus some territories now in neighbouring states, including Mount Ararat ('Masis' to most Armenians). Did they think they were heading to Armenia? *From* 'Armenia', as their homeland was known? We Armenians call it 'Western Armenia'. Such was the fate of the Armenian Highlands – subjected to carve-ups by empires since antiquity – that our sense of geographic congruence is mangled. What is it like to say your country's name and see one well-defined physical entity? Is it important, such clarity about the contours of one's homeland?

Ashkhen's father, Yeranos, was a land-owning farmer. They had domestic workers, as my mother heard from childhood. A wet-nurse may have breast-fed Great-grandma. They must have lived with an extended family in their village near modern-day Erzurum. Its name is lost to us. I've no clue what other relatives they had, lost, or lost touch with. Someone reading this in France could be my distant cousin. Or, was the rich landowner in fact her grandfather? All we know is she was born into an affluent household.

On the tape, she says they heard constant gunfire (WWI was on): Eeh, *tupu-tupu-tupu-tupu*. Russo–Turkish fighting, with Armenians – as it happened and continues to happen with the colonised and divided peoples – on both sides. Eastern Armenians and Western Armenians, Russo–Armenians and Turko–Armenians.

My mother:

– Do you remember your father, tati?

– No. He had taken flour to Arzirum... and went and went.

Meaning that was it, he never returned. I assume he'd taken flour to sell as a wholesaler. *Arzirum* and not 'Erzrum'? It was Arzrum to Pushkin, who had visited decades prior, as part of his Caucasian journey, after the region's Russian conquest (Were Ashkhen's ancestors bothered?). Way back, to the olden-day natives, it was Karin-city.

Did the Turks or the Kurds kidnap her father, rob him, then release him? Did they forcefully convert him, or kill him? No hard facts. I recall hearing that Èva had buried 'gold' in the ground before fleeing (money, or jewellery?), but this practice was common, so I'm not sure. Ashkhen does say: Mother lost wads of gold, left it on trains and in carriages during pakhepakh. To translate with precision would be tricky, but 'pakhnel' means 'to run away'. The repetition of 'pakh' and 'pakh' makes it sound like *rush-and-run*. I've only ever heard it used in the context of the Genocide, by ordinary people.

For all my pride in our extant family history, for all their eagerness to hand it down, I am in a fog about it. So much is eradicated in the process, or generated, so much is erased by chance. I do not know if their village had been raided, if they were chased by a mob, if they saw anything gruesome en route, or if anything nasty was done to them. Did a Kurdish or Turkish family hide them? It may explain Ashkhen's absence of hatred.

Flashback: her torn earlobe (who pulled her gold earring?), her small body (under-nourishment?), her smell, her beady eyes, her fingernails with ridges (vitamin deficiency?), the way she played with my hair – softly, monotonously scratching my head at bedtime, making a scraping sound. Her own hair, limp and long, exposed exclusively for combing and washing.

Did she ever go to a hairdresser? This ancestor of mine, once-alive bridge to the times all but gone, disappeared.

❀

Even if I had basic coordinates, I have little desire to find their place. Those coordinates don't determine me. Should I go to Eastern Anatolia, or Western Armenia, like some diasporan Armenians, or my friends or their parents from Armenia have done, it wouldn't be 'our' house. Nor would I be a vengeful claimant. Yet feeling an emotional attachment to the area, I do fear finding it painful. Would that make me a nostalgic pilgrim?

Off the cart, and got on a 'train', she says. The Kars–Alexandropol, presumably. As I type, Word auto-correct suggests 'Mars', but Armenian-speakers pronounce it 'Ghars', as in 'r' in 'bonjour'. The railway had been laid in the 1890s to connect (and control) the newly conquered Russian South Caucasus. It ran from Kars (now Turkey) to Alexandropol (now Gyumri, Armenia), and on to Tiflis (now Tbilisi, Georgia). All three were imperial Russian possessions back then. On the train, Èva traded a silver belt for a loaf of black bread, I've repeatedly heard. It must still exist – someone out there must cherish this heirloom, this kyamar, handed down by their railway guard ancestor, or, more likely, by his wife.

Most likely, they got off at Alexandropol. A major hub and destination for most, it was named so by a visiting tsar (or tzar, or czar?) after his wife, Alexandra (formerly, Princess Charlotte of Prussia). In Soviet times, it was Leninakan, re-named – no surprise – after Lenin. Anyway, the gubernia was throbbing with refugees, including Assyrians and Greeks, from the empire on the other side.

Vivacious, epicurean, larger-than-life, Gyumri (Kumayri to Armenians from time immemorial) was by all accounts the cultural capital. Soon, it would come to be known, spine-chillingly, as the 'city of orphans' or orphan-city: at least ten institutions based there housed over 30,000 genocide orphans, including on the site of the abandoned Russian garrison, well into the 1920s. Reading this makes me halt my hunt for the photograph. So, from my grandmother's generation down to mine, with our roots but no shoots in Western Armenia, we were raised by a pull of forebears who themselves didn't have proper parents, let alone grandparents?! Over 20,000 names are preserved in the archives. If we knew Ashkhen's maiden name, I might find it written down. If she was there.

Where did Èva, Ashkhen – and whoever was left from their group – go from Empress Alexandra's town? Silence. Èva found a job at an orphanage as a washerwoman, as per the recording, so that her one living child would be fed and housed – in the same place.

In her few years of schooling (were the classes orphanage-run?), Ashkhen often played truant, tells my mother, refusing to go to class because bullies – local Armenians – called her a 'smelly refugee'. Is that why she remained semi-literate? Or, worse still, a self-confessed անգրագետ գեղացի կին: illiterate village woman. Inferior on all three counts. Prior to massacres, might she have studied at one of the missionary-run colleges, sprung up in the ailing, deep Anatolia?

Thankfully, wisdom does not only land on the learned.

❦

The year Armenia became part of the USSR, Èva, then in her late forties, accepted an offer of marriage. Being blue-eyed, tall, regal and organised, Èva had many suitors, my mother heard. Did they notice the Tsarist collapse, the 1918 restoration of statehood after long ages, wars with the neighbours, Bolshevik invasion and take-over of the nascent republic? More shifting (shrinking) of borders, Armenians losing Masis, being caught in the deals between the successors of empires on either side – including one signed in the Prussian Princess' town, another in Kars/Mars? In between there was civil strife, plus Transcaucasian federations (I confuse the dates but we're talking months). Now *you* are confused, as well. Overall, less than ten years since their escape, being caught in the storm's evil eye.

I don't know if Ashkhen's step-father was a former Ottoman subject (Western Armenian). Surely, a brave widower, taking on as his wife somebody with a broken past. On the tape: when he died, he'd been married to Èva for forty-five years. Did they, mother and daughter ever search for their husband and father, missing others? Did they miss their shared past – the *before*, the old country? Did they store it away in a file separate from the new life?

Now stabilised, Èva collected Ashkhen from the orphanage (which?), bringing her to the man's house in Kurtan (still there, name unchanged). On the tape, my mother:

– Gran, did Vartan love Èva?

– He was besotted, vuy, how embarrassing.

My father:

– Was Èva beautiful, Gran?

She slows down, as if gifting a pearl, and then, not as a daughter about her mother, but as a woman about another woman:

– Very beautiful.

My mother, who knew them in childhood, recently re-established contact with Èva's adopted family in Kurtan. Vartan's grand-children took her to her great-grandmother's grave, praising Èva to the skies as tall, blue-eyed, regal, and organised. No mention of her ever talking about their previous life to her Eastern Armenian step-family. Afterwards, a mono-chrome image arrived via Facebook: Èva, surrounded by her post-carnage clan, black headscarf, eye-balling the camera. It is saved on my laptop; I must digitise Ashkhen's photo as well, once I've found it.

Èva, my grandmother's grandmother, was still alive when I was small, but to me, she's an alien. Her daughter, on the other hand, is kin. I keep meaning to say that the 'kh' in tati's name is pronounced like the Spanish 'j' in 'Juan'.

Her stepfather, Vartan, and his children were nice. But her mother was eager to see her get married. On that sole trace of her voice we have: Mother married me off, to have my own place and family. She said, you'll be left with these strangers if I die. But she didn't die, did she? Chuckle. Married off, if my maths adds up, within two years of settling in Kurtan, to go live with *other* strangers, after Sukias knocked on the door with his uncle to ask for her hand. She was younger than my teenage daughter now. He – over fifteen years her senior. Admittedly, a fellow genocide survivor, because: Èva wouldn't have a local beat me up and curse, You smelly refugee. Because wives would expect to be beaten. He had seen her once at his relative's, their neighbour's. I was knitting a sharp. A scarf.

❁

This business of remembrance is proving hard. I want to weave these stories with my own, to bridge the gap between our time and theirs. But as I try to hand down 'solid material', as I dig from this distance, more gaps – linguistic, cultural – keep emerging.

۞

Child bride Ashkhen entered Dsegh village (not far from Kurtan), on a horse, courtesy of her groom's employer, wearing a dress on loan, moving into the employer's home, where Sukias had been lodging. Dsegh's most famous son for all times, Hovhannes Tumanyan, had not long died. Had Ashkhen heard of his tragic poem about Maro, another child? On the recording, she is cheerful and confident: Master was a rich man but very nice. Rich but nice, echoes my mother. No wavering, chuckle. His gift to the newly-weds was bedding. In return for a year's labour, he'd also taken care of the wedding expenses. I got up the next day, wore that dress, but the master's wife said, it's the neighbour's.

My mother:

– Poor thing, you were only fourteen.

– I learnt quick, though: Ճարպիկ էի: I didn't dilly-dally.

If I wanted to, I could not trace their steps today. Kars–Leninakan became an inter-state railroad with the Bolshevik–Turkish border shift (called 'treaty'). It kept running in Soviet times, shutting in the early '90s, a time of privations where I come from – due to the Spitak earthquake, Soviet collapse, Nagorno-Karabakh war (the First), and the resulting economic blockade. The Gyumri–Tbilisi line is operational, and from Kars, one can reach Tbilisi, albeit in a roundabout way. As for the Kurtan to Dsegh village-to-village stretch, I can do that, as my daughter has.

On the tape, unaware she is being recorded, Ashkhen briefly becomes an interviewer. To my mother:

– Your father didn't hit your mother, did he?

– No. Did your husband beat you up, Gran?

– Absolutely not. Your Grandad was kind, shame he died young.

Sukias, my quiet, book-loving great-grandfather, was no wife-beater. He was a noqyar, she uses Turkish, a manservant. The girl who'd had servants, married a servant. A noqyar, whose father also hadn't survived the pakhepakh. In what way was he damaged? Genocide, gender leveller, renders men worthless, I hear. He couldn't afford a wedding band.

Aged twenty-two (or twenty-four?), she gave birth to my grandmother Seda, her youngest child, in the employer's house. I recall she had also miscarried. Was there stillbirth, besides? I ought to check with Mamà, but with so much I'm checking already, there'll be no time for a conversation. Thus we find out we do not know our origins.

They kept moving: Eeh, dog's life, moving from so-and-so's place to so-and-so's.

Anyway, Yerevan is my grandmother's place of birth. It became the Armenian capital – throughout history there've been over a dozen – with the first independent republic, but was truly developed (herein lies the irony of fate) in the short decades after, throughout Soviet '20s and '30s. In those blackest of times – go figure – Yerevan was a hotbed of culture: of that cohort of Russo– and Turko–Armenians, many orphans. When did Ashkhen and Sukias make it to Yerevan? Simple folk of the land, were they driven out of the countryside by the brute kolektivizatsia? Or pulled *into* the capital by the neck-breaking industrializatsia?

❋

Flashback: Ashkhen's agile hands. Sifting spelt from chaff, stone from buckwheat, cooking with lard, and washing the carpets every steady hot Yerevan summer.

That was an undertaking. Women brought carpets out, hose pipes, washing powder, and an all-wooden mop – to push the soapy water out. It was no broom with tough bristles, as the Google images show. Back inside the flats, as a child, I watched women wrap a wet rag around its head to clean lacquered wooden floors or tiled ones, and a dry one for mastika'd parquet. It was nowhere near the 'magic' mops from Vileda with sponge or with refills of microfibre, available in Armenia these days. Now it occurs to me that I probably never saw Ashkhen do the carpets: it was heavy work, and she wasn't young.

She did 'whip up the wools', however, a regular task in a place at a time when bedding cost money. Araxie's so rich that her wools are stacked, ooh, this high, she said. Every couple of years, covers were undone, lambswool extracted, one mattress or duvet at a time, washed in a bath, dried on sheets in the scorching sun, fluffed up with a stick, then stuffed back into covers and sewn to keep the stuffing evenly distributed. I can call up the smell of wet wool (sheep, really) in a heartbeat. Or the sight of the down, washed in bowls or buckets. Once dried, it would fly everywhere, so we children would gather it up, and tati would stuff it in pillow cases, seal, and *tup-tup-tup*. A woman's work is never finished, sweetheart.

This back-breaking practice, which the spoiled me has been spared, which an immigrant from Armenia tried to keep alive outside her LA condominium in the 2000s (who was swiftly referred to mental health services by her Californian neighbours), is dying out. Good. But I'm frustrated about mining to find its descriptions, depictions, and to prove its existence in English.

There is one video (in Armenian) on YouTube, where a woman bemoans the lazy new generation for choosing hollowfibre over all-natural, hand-treated woollen bedding for winters. It was called 'sindipon' in Armenia, but my desktop research brings up 'Sintepon'. What else have I taken for granted that may turn out otherwise?

❀

Second World War fighting didn't reach Armenia, but Armenians were enlisted into the Red Army. Sukias, too old for combat, was called up as a cook, if memory serves. How long was he away for? Rummaging for tati's photo, I'd rather not stop-and-start so as to verify. Mum says that he reached Germany, and on return, raved about the homes he'd seen there: every single one had a washing machine and a great many books, apparently.

During the war, Ashkhen worked at a grain storage and milling facility. Zakozerno is still there – surprise – in Yerevan's outskirts, as the web shows. Zakozerno stands for 'Zakavkazskoye zerno' in Russian, or 'Transcaucasian grain'. Doesn't 'za' in the word 'Zakavkazye' (Transcaucasia) signify 'past/across from/beyond/on the other side' of the Caucasus? So my region was named from the north, from the Russian side. Should it be '*Pre*caucasia' now?

Every night before going home, Zakozerno workers, overwhelmingly women, were frisked. And one day Ashkhen was caught thieving. A young guard found a bag of flour under her clothes. He said, Put it back, apparently. Note this was Stalin's USSR, where you could be sent to the gulag, or shot for this kind of crime. Did she do it often? Did they all do it? I wouldn't be surprised.

There was a famine in the South Caucasus, 'disease and famine', as per Wikipedia. I'd never heard of it. That doesn't surprise me, either. We do not know half of our history. Her mischievous voice is ringing in my ear: I said, Let me go, son, I've got three hungry children at home. Here, take the half, don't shop me please.

'Son', said a woman just over thirty. Would she resent our carefree living, seventy-is-the-new-forty, apparently? Or begrudge us taking our privileges for granted? She, who saw deportation, dead siblings, chaos, hunger, revolt, world wars, near-seventy years of Communism (did it ever arrive?), other contingency – all the stuff history's made from.

❋

Her daughter, my grandmother Seda, was a prolific seamstress, but I don't recall Ashkhen tati sewing. She would have mended, as my mother did: life was hard, people pinched kopecks to get by. A woman's right hand should steal from the left, sweetheart.

Flashback: she's staying with us during school holidays, I'm being sent up the mount behind our building with my brother. Pick some thyme, stinging nettles, kids – and sorrel. I will lay them to dry in the sun, that's your winter soup sorted.

I remember the aluminium meat grinder she bought my mother, squeezing her meagre pension in the good (well, better) days of Brezhnev. And the set of gold-plated teaspoons, *my* only material possession from her. For your dowry: օժիտ. (That word, ozhit, anachronistic and out of context.) Whenever you use it, you'll remember me, sweetheart. Chuckle.

What to do with their art of economising, their talent for a dinner party spread with a handful of products, like my mother's during war and blockade and rationing?

I might die without imparting these ways to my daughter. Would she want them? Did Ashkhen fear the same? Keep stirring the yoghurt with a wooden spoon over low heat so your spass (or spas) isn't curdled, she taught me, certain that it was something essential, something that would equip me for the future. In my half-a-life spent in England, I have made that traditional yoghurt soup of whole wheat grains, egg yoke, and herbs just once. For various reasons, it's vacated my mental cookbook.

She never showed her ankles; her dresses were black or brown – a round neck, straight, loose cut, long sleeves, no frills. Yet, she praised my mother for dressing us and herself according to the latest fashions. Well done, Goldenhands. Was she driven by progress or pleasure? She'd be proud of my education, though in her times, studious women were suspect. And, why kid ourselves; where she came from, women covered their mouths laughing, stood up when a male relative entered, and, Bring your knees together, my girl.

I tell my daughter the same. In response, she briefly spreads them wider.

There is much that I don't know. At some stage, Ashkhen and Sukias with the three children lived in what in my youth was fondly remembered as 'the gorge house'. A full district of shacks on river Hrazdan's craggy slopes in the capital. Did they have electricity there in the 1950s? Did they wash in the river? Carry water up from Hrazdan?

The images I have of her – not few – leave gaps for interpretation. For instance, the tablets she took, which we called 'noshpa' ('NO-SPA', apparently); I can see them, even smell them. Were they for blood pressure or migraine? On some mornings she said: I woke up in the night, went after a thought and lost sleep. Then claimed that standing under a cold shower would get rid of her *heavy head* (depression?). What thoughts did she pursue? Did they hound *her*?

And I hear her sorrowful singing – as if overcome, grief-struck. Time, for me, slowed down to a standstill, as she sang herself to a whimper, then – blinded by the burning tears – wiped them with the back of her hand, holding on to the knife, and continued peeling potatoes. Improvised, enigmatic songs: 'Let's go back to our country'. Also about the 'the evil fate of my little son'.

❦

Hrachya (Uncle Hrach to us) was her eldest child, who had been left deaf and mute by a childhood illness. Eventually he had married someone like himself, and they'd had three children (after losing two) with perfect hearing, raised mainly by Ashkhen. He and his wife worked, I've no idea where. In the summer of 1973 or '74, their two children were returning from a visit to their other grandmother, on a train Yerevan-bound, planning to join their parents and sister, then head up to the Black Sea for a holiday with friends of their parents.

The train crashed headlong into another one, and among those killed were the two children, a boy and a girl, each under twenty; only their body parts were found. Had they lived long enough to see me, they'd be my Uncle

Hakob and Aunt Alvard. So Ahkhen, the bereaved doting grandmother and a mother who was reeling for her bereaved child.

I cannot find a reference to the accident online, in Armenian, Russian, or English. It's a safe bet that the Soviets hid it. When recovering from this surgery of mine, I'll have time to dig around properly.

By the time I knew him, Uncle Hrach was always subdued at family parties: a gentle smile, sign language, people fussing over him on the margins. He'd been divorced for years, his marriage rocked by the loss of the children. People said he was not the same.

Much of what befell them remains a sealed mystery. If I met them as adults, I would ask how hard it was, pushing the figurative cart of life forward, lugging it round, resigned, wounded, and downcast. Did Great-grandmother want to 'vanish, become invisible', like my own mother when she lost *her* grandchild? Did she say what my mother told me: Not to die, lest I hurt you, but to seamlessly cease existing? Even if they resisted destiny, did they feel broken? I hope I'd maintain a fondness for them. There's always the chance that I might disappoint them. We subsequent generations are strange creatures, not quite familial. Confined in our time as they were inextricable from theirs, maybe to them, *we* are the trapped.

Here's the thing, though: I remember tati distraught, going through an avalanche of sadness, though never once morose or bitter. A survivor, did her veins contain steel? And I heard her pray (God, to her, still existed). As if balancing hope with anxiety, she would whisper. Did despair ever prevail? Did it threaten to swallow? Would she chuckle at us problem-fixers? Would she say: Some problems aren't for solving; they should just be endured, sweetheart. Tati jan, how about 'what ifs'?

Hrachya died – of a broken heart, or old age (in his fifties?!), or an illness. I remember being tasked with sorting through his postcards. He was friends with a group of deaf people from the Baltics, visited Latvia (or Estonia), and had a correspondence with a lady. A telegram would have notified her of his passing; did she telegram back commiserations?

Great-grandmother was a widow; Sukias, her husband, had returned from the war but was long dead. And I watched her, a feather-light character, curled up on the balcony couch, staring at a spot in the air, fondling prayer beads, thoughts vacating her, then language: Թողանայի, այս չտեսար: 'God strike me blind rather than let me see this.' Or, mid-jobs, mind taking flight, you'd think, to another dimension, only sorrowful whimpers betraying her presence, breaking into laments, always starting with 'my poor Hrachig, Hrachig jan'. Note the diminutive 'ig', pronounced in Western Armenian. The diminutive in my pronunciation, my mother's and my grandmother Seda's would be 'ik', a harder, Eastern Armenian sound (another legacy of partitions). Nothing, they say, but a patchwork tapestry, our language has two branches, plus dozens of dialects. Or it did before massacres, modernisatsia, and migration. Did the gap between hers and all of our vernacular bother her?

In that shared past of ours, a fortunate life was one in which parents didn't bury their kids. 'I hope you leave this world with a dry eye' went the saying (still goes), which implies no tears shed for the loss of one's child. Everything else either doesn't warrant tears or is surmountable; they will dry. So, her laments ended with 'lucky Sukias', since her husband, having died with a dry eye, didn't lose his son. Although – a puzzle – I've also heard her mumble: I've cried so much, I've run out of tears.

Where are my origins? In Turkey (where both sides on my maternal line come from), in Iran (where at least one side of my paternal line comes from) or today's Armenia, one more lost homeland?

Great-grandmother's was the first funeral I remember. All her (living) grandchildren and great-grandchildren were present. In that February 1988, I was younger than my daughter now (she's met no great-grandparent on either side). Were the pro-Karabakh demonstrations pounding Opera Square?

Given what she had witnessed, Ashkhen lived a thousand years.

So many people came to her flat. The mirrors were draped with black cloth, the coffin was on the table in the centre of the living room, and close female relatives sat in the front row. Guests filed past to pay death due respect, stopping by the deceased's nearest, embracing and wishing them patience. They always say that Աստված քեզ համբերություն տա: God give you patience. But patience for what, until when?! Could it be, with yourself?

Many leant forward to kiss her. I stroked her hands crossed on her chest, crying. She was wearing the clothes prepared for this occasion. This was widespread; women put aside outfits for their own wakes and their husbands', hiding cash for their funerals under mattresses. Ashkhen had done that with Èva, too. On the recording: When Khrushov changed the money, not to lose it, Mother and I went to spend the thousand rubli I'd saved up, bought some fabric, a pair of sleepers, her funeral clothing... and this wedding ring for me. Chuckle.

Tati took a great deal to the grave with her, and I'm fumbling for it blindly as I root around. What would she say of my moving away? Of my going and going. And the haemorrhage of the exodus that dispatched overseas half of her grandchildren and great-grandchildren, scattered her address book contacts like washed and dried wool and down?

In turn, I'll take *my* deepest: that I could not love my children more but I'm unable to show it better; that from this country of plenty, I feel greedy for roads not taken; and the fact that I'm scared of dying now, though my little son did it first, on his own.

Have I been doing her justice here? In those yesterdays of ours, bleeding onto the page like this was a no-no. Fate could give so much worse. It has spared me pakhepakh. Hence adults said: Կյանք ա. That is life, which implies anything happens, no surprise, just be dignified. So Ashkhen may refuse her portrayal as long-suffering. Life, to her, may have worked out regardless.

After all, what was a woman then? A superman.

How strange that she's a stranger to my daughter. Who adores spass, prepared by my mother, which is my small triumph. Over what? Getting lost, being broken, forgetting. Not broken psychologically – soup is a small loss. Broken down into parentheses or inadequate translations or quotation marks or forward slashes or approximations or italicised foreign words or poor analogies or internet search results or irregular transliterations or spelling suggestions or name changes. A victory therefore over becoming a discontinuous, disjointed being. Not merely hyphenated, but ruptured, incoherent to myself, with a mangled sense of history, severed in my life's temporal flow, my narration of events, narration never finished.

I'm now older than my grandmother Seda was when I was my daughter's age, older than she was when she became a grandmother. Older than my mother was when I got married. All of us have seen wars and rationing. Like Ashkhen, I will die with 'a wet eye'. Should it happen during this surgery, my mother will share that fate. Like Ashkhen and her mother Èva, I'll be buried far from my place of origin and my foremothers' graves, in my son's shared spot in London – ever the same nation's capital, with its name unchanged for just shy of a thousand years, and its well-defined borders, uncontested, unclaimed since long.

❦

What processes would my death trigger in my daughter? It will teach me to give up control, to let her who comes after us make her world. Will she shed habits, cede beliefs, put her stamp on which things? Would she carry on, blissfully distancing from her origins, except those perhaps whom she saw alive, me and her grandmother? Would she deem some forgetfulness useful, besides being inevitable?

She might start reading Armenian books manically, tracing my steps while she can visit *this* Armenia, in current borders. She might falter, check if I did Arabic or Persian at university, get the chronology wrong. Contact people via Facebook, people I wouldn't want to hear about my death or to be in touch with. Of course that can be its own kind of forgetting. Doesn't memory accommodate what fits the narrative most easily?

Which of my sayings would ring in her ears? Will I have taught her anything useful? What possessions of mine will she treasure? Will she criticise or understand my mending: Why did she waste time darning socks, we were not on the breadline? Will she say: I had no dowry, I just received stories. Mamà loved language. Or, like a woman speaking about a woman: She was beautiful?

Who can say. I don't plan to ask her. But I hope that she'll be free of unease or anxiety – about the gap between her cultures, about her maternal side from another planet, and about their ways, anachronistic to this other. That she'll name those who raised her and translate the concepts that made her with confidence, no wavering. That she'll never utter a 'smelly refugee' about others, nor herself be called that, ever. And that, should I die during my procedure, she will keep this picture of me, flanked by defiant witnesses to an antique, traumatic era, this sepia photo – atelier Gagik – found filed away in my 'Armenia' album.

Naneh V Hovhannisyan is an Armenian-born writer of book reviews, essays, and memoir pieces. She is interested in history, memory, and belonging. In 2018, she was selected by Writing West Midlands for the Room 204 Emerging Writer Development scheme. Her work has been published by *EVN Report*, *WritersMosaic*, *Wasafiri* and the *Cambridge Review of Books*, among others. A short story of hers featured in the West Midlands Readers' Networks' 2021 anthology, *New Stories for Readers*, and her article series, *Breaking Bread with Neighbours*, was published by the Armenian Institute, London. Naneh co-edited the 2024 special issue of *Wasafiri* (120) on Armenian Writing, and is working on her first book and its accompanying radio programmes.

A new magazine featuring the very best prose from Wales – and beyond

ISSUE 001: ROOTS - OUT NOW

ISSUE 002: SPEAK TO ME - COMING JULY

Go to **foldingrock.com**
to subscribe

🐦 📘 📷 @FoldingRockMag

Visit our webs

Submit your w

THE DOCKS

SARAH LENER

RIFKA LIES AWAKE WHILE HER HUSBAND AVI SLEEPS. HE TWITCHES and fidgets sometimes flinging a leg, sometimes an arm, towards her side of the bed. He gets this way when money worries are bad.

She moves across to the far side of the bed and curls up on her side, her back facing Avi. She can't stop thinking about Mama and Leah. Their letter said they'd be here for Rosh Ha Shona hopefully, and by Yom Kippur for certain. In August she went to the docks to meet the boat from Hamburg but there was no sign of them. The September boat will dock today, and Yom Kippur begins tomorrow. By now they must be close to the coast of Wales, huddled together on deck, their puchs stretched over them for warmth.

The clock strikes four. It's too early but she climbs out of bed and splashes her face with cold water. She dresses quickly and brushes her hair, now streaked with grey. Her hair was bright ginger once, thick, and long enough to sell. She closes her eyes and feels the cold metal of scissors against her skin.

On the way to the outhouse, she passes the workshop. She opens the door quietly. Four workers sleep under the benches. The air is stale with their sweat and full of stench from the steam iron. Avi says he can't afford to pay them any more money. They're gruner – still learning the trade. When she gets home, she'll make them coffee with plenty of sugar. She leaves the door open to change the air.

In the kitchen she lights the stove so there's warmth for the household, makes tea and cuts a slice of bread but she's too on edge to eat. She leaves the bread on a plate and covers it with a saucer for later.

She tightens her headscarf, pulls her shawl around her, and leaves the house. It's still dark and the street is quiet. A breeze blows from the embankment where in summer she likes to wander. Sorrel grows here. She uses it to keep her family healthy. It was a miracle the first time she saw it here in Cardiff, the sight taking her back to riverbanks near Gorodets where it had grown so plentifully. She and Leah used to swim in that river on hot summer evenings before Shabbat. They'd be with a group of other girls, hiding from the boys and splashing each other as they suppressed shrieks of laughter. Next summer she'll take Mama and Leah to Barry. They've never had a day out by the sea. She and Leah will swim, and Leah will be astonished at the way the saltwater helps a person float. Mama will have her stockings peeled off, the sand between her toes.

She walks quickly to the main street and waits for the first tram to the docks. A couple of other people are waiting, also. They eye her curiously. She still looks foreign with her long, coloured skirt and scarf, but she isn't as wary of the locals as she used to be.

The tram arrives and she climbs on board, sitting alone at the back where no one will bother her. Her stomach rumbles and she feels under her skirts for a sweet. She finds a gobstopper, one of her favourites.

Going to the docks used to be a big adventure all those years ago. For a long time Avi's tailoring business had been hand to mouth. Then one day an official letter arrived. It was an offer of a contract to make uniforms for the Cardiff Tramway Corporation. Avi turned to her, pale-faced, almost frightened. "We haven't got enough workers, Rifka," he said.

That's when she started going to the docks. She went all over the place, to Cardiff, Hull and Liverpool, collecting poor Jews from everywhere: Russia, Poland and Germany. Mostly they slept under the benches in the workshop till they learned their trade.

Now Avi has lost the Tramway contract – and they don't need any more workers.

More people board the tram, others like her, going to the docks, for what purpose she isn't certain. Outside it's still dark. The gobstopper melts in her mouth.

On Rosh Ha Shona, with no Mama and Leah, she had swallowed her disappointment, hoping for a good year, and a sweet one, as she dipped her apple in honey. She looked around her table. Her younger son Sol sat a few places down. He's a hard-working boy. Soon he'll be a skilled tailor. Eli, her oldest boy, was absent as usual. He ran off to work in a fairground at the age of fourteen and they hardly ever saw him. It was years since he'd been with the family for Rosh ha Shona. Perhaps it was her own fault that he had turned out so badly. She had uprooted him when he was so little, pulling him away from his beloved granny and auntie. It was different for Sol, he was only a tiny baby when they'd left Russia – he didn't know what was happening. She hoped that when Mama and Leah arrived, Eli would visit and be happy to see them. If he refused to come home, or was cold and indifferent, she didn't think she could bear it.

Ach but Sadie, her oldest girl sat at her right hand – her hair brown like the honey cake they made for dessert. Sadie's not just pretty but clever also. Perhaps one day she'll work in an office. Next to Sadie was Rosa – thirteen and already surrounded by boys, red haired and headstrong. You wouldn't think she hadn't walked for a year, after that accident with the carpet when she was only five. Further down the table, clustered together, was a handful of workers. Rifka couldn't leave them on Yomtov with nowhere to go.

Avi sat opposite her at the far end of the table. Next to him was his father Heime – grey haired and frail now, hardly aware of his surroundings, reciting the Hebrew prayers to himself silently under his breath. He comes to life only when he goes to the workshop to swap stories from home. She's always had a little feeling of resentment that Avi brought Heime from Russia before she could send for Mama and Leah. She'll be able to forget all that when Mama and Leah arrive.

They reach the docks, the end of the line. The tram empties, the other passengers disappear into the dark. She pulls her shawl around her and goes to the place where the boats from Hamburg arrive. Out there in the estuary are waiting ships. She can almost feel them looming in the dark but they won't approach the harbour until dawn. She smells the sea on the wind. Gulls circle overhead, screeching in the air.

A seaman stands nearby, coiling a rope around his arm. He was here before.

'They've not docked yet, bach – shouldn't be long now.'

She smiles, her stomach tightens.

More people arrive. A group of women have crosses around their necks. She's seen what they do. They offer help, but also conversion. The waiting men are worse. The young girls arriving alone will likely trust them because they speak Yiddish. G-d knows if they really are Jews or what those girls will have to do in exchange for food in their bellies and a roof over their heads. She stands apart. There's a limit to the number of people you can help. It isn't like it used to be when they had money and now there are also debts from Avi's gambling.

She hates it when men come to the house to play cards. She hears their voices from the kitchen; sometimes there's laughter, but also long silences, and voices raised in anger. The next morning Avi will be pale, eyes sunken, and that week there'll be no money for housekeeping. Sometimes he'll tell some of the workers to leave. It breaks her when that happens.

Luckily, she has always been careful with money, kept some back in the good times. When she got the letter from Leah telling her about the group leaving from Kobrin, she couldn't believe it. Finally, it was going happen – Mama and Leah would leave Russia. She had rushed straight upstairs and uncovered the jar she kept hidden in the back of the wardrobe. She had been saving for years and now she had enough money for their tickets. They would come by train and then by ship. She couldn't afford a cabin for them, though; they'd be out on the open deck. They'd carry their possessions rolled up in their puchs so they'd have to unpack if they wanted to use the puchs for warmth.

The light changes, the dark becomes grey. The ships approach slowly, and one comes towards the waiting group, the ship that carries Mama and Leah, with the group from Kobrin.

As soon as the boat docks she pushes her way on board and makes for the lower deck. There's a group of poor Jews looking around them, excited and confused. She rushes towards them, stepping over crates and ropes. Mama and Leah aren't among them.

A tall man looks at her, his wife and children are behind him. 'What place is this?' he asks in Yiddish.

'This is the town of Cardiff in south Wales,' she says.

'But we have tickets for America. Does this ship go to America?'

'I doubt it. You'll have to ask someone – tell me, where are you from?'

'We are from Brest, in Belarus.'

'That is not so far from my area. Are there people here from Kobrin?'

He indicates with his head towards a group standing some yards away.

'I must talk to them,' she says. 'One of the men down on the dock will tell you if the ship is going to America. If you go to Chicago, I have a brother there, Reuben Kaufmann. Tell him to help you. Say his sister Rifka sent you.'

The man nods, but still looks worried.

She pushes on, looking for Mama and Leah.

A young woman sits alone holding her baby.

'Excuse me,' Rifka asks her, 'Are you from Kobrin?'

'Yes,' the woman looks exhausted.

'I'm looking for my mother and sister, Sarah and Leah Kaufmann, two women travelling alone. Have you seen them?'

The woman shakes her head. 'No, I haven't seen them. I don't think they're with us. There aren't two women travelling alone.'

This young woman is stupid.

'But they must be, they were definitely going to travel with you. I sent them tickets. They are from our stetl, Gorodets.'

'Ah, Gorodets.'

'Yes, surely you know them?'

'I don't know them, but I have cousins in Gorodets. I'd remember if I met someone from there.'

'Is someone in charge of your group?'

The woman points to a gentle-faced young man. He's surrounded by landsleit asking him questions. She must queue to speak to him.

'My mother and sister were meant to join you, Sarah and Leah Kaufman. Do you know them?'

'Yes. I remember, they were due to join us, but they didn't arrive. Something must have gone wrong at the last minute. It happens.'

'But I sent them tickets.'

'There will be other opportunities. Next year, my brother will come. He will lead a group of people.'

She can't believe Mama and Leah would have wasted the precious tickets, but she thinks ahead.

'How can I contact your brother?'

The man tears a scrap of paper from a notebook and scrawls a name, and an address.

As she leaves the ship, she passes the young woman. 'Do you have somewhere to go?' she asks.

'Not yet.'

'How can you have travelled alone with a young baby and no one to go to?'

'My husband left for England, but I haven't heard from him. I am trying to find him.'

She's heard many stories like this – men who leave and never send for their families.

'This is Wales, not England,' she says.

The woman's face wobbles.

'England isn't too far away,' Rifka adds quickly. 'Just the other side of the water.'

On the dock are those Christian women, those lecherous men.

Rifka had travelled from Russia with no husband and two young children but at least Avi was waiting for them when they'd finally arrived. She doesn't see how this woman and baby will manage.

She reaches into her pocket and takes out some coins from her housekeeping money. Avi will never know.

'Here's some money,' she says to the woman thrusting the coins in her hand. 'Try to stay with the others from your group until you find somewhere to stay. And there are men on the dock who speak Yiddish. Don't go with them, they are bad people.'

She moves away from the woman. She has done all she can.

On the way off the boat, she sees the tall man from Brest arguing with an official in broken English. His wife and two children, a boy and a girl are with him. She wishes she could do something for him.

When she gets home Avi is sitting at the kitchen table with Heime. Sadie and Rosa are clearing up after the midday meal. Both Rosa and Avi have sullen expressions. Perhaps they've had a row before she arrived – they are so alike: strong willed and stubborn.

'Nu?' Avi says when he sees her.

'They weren't there.'

Avi frowns. 'There must be a simple explanation.'

'Try not to worry,' Heime says in a quavering voice.

She remembers that day when Rosa wouldn't go to school. Avi had shouted and yelled. Rosa cried and bawled but still she wouldn't go. Avi had dragged her across the floor. Her leg got caught up with the loose carpet in the hallway and twisted in its socket. The child could have been crippled for life.

Rifka looks directly at Avi, avoiding Heime's gaze. 'We could have sent for them before, but you kept saying we didn't have the money. You brought your own father, but not my family.'

'Rifka...' he says.

She doesn't listen.

She rushes down to the embankment and stares at the river. Avi never said sorry for what he did to Rosa – though Rifka knows he felt guilty. She saw it in his eyes. A whole year the child lay in bed. Then one day a gypsy woman came to the house selling her wares and they got talking. Rifka told the woman about Rosa. 'You must get a cactus and put the juice on her leg,' the woman told her. Avi snorted when Rifka did as the woman said, 'Cactus juice? Really? Why do you believe this woman when the doctors can do nothing?'

A week later, Rosa had walked again.

On Kol Nidre, Rifka schlepps fish from the market as usual and chops it on the kitchen table banging down with her hackmesser. She'll leave the gefullte fish ready to break the fast. For dinner that evening she makes chicken soup with noodles. Filling enough to sustain them, but not too heavy. The rich smell wafts out of the kitchen – it will reach the workshop. She's twice as busy as usual. Thank G-d there's no time to think.

As night falls, she and Avi lead their household to Schul. She goes up to the women's gallery with Sadie and Rosa, her two girls who Mama and Leah have never met.

The melodies fill her mind. They come to the Al Chet Prayer:

> For the sins we have committed before you under duress, or willingly and for the sin we have committed before you by hard heartedness....

Maybe Mama and Leah are lost on some frozen waste, or perhaps they were arrested crossing one of the borders. They'd have no idea how to cope if that happened, how to bargain or manoeuvre, and they'd have no money for a bribe.

'How can you do this?' Leah had asked, when Rifka said she was leaving Russia to join Avi in England. Leah clutched Sol in her arms. Mama pressed Eli against her. He hid his face in Mama's skirts, she stroked his head.

'You can't go with these two,' Mama said, 'what will happen to them? You can't manage them alone.'

'The Rabbi said I won't be alone. The Jewish people are always together. That's what he told me.'

'The Rabbi? Has he helped you in this?' Mama asked.

'No, Mama, it isn't like that.'

'You've always been selfish,' Leah said, her eyes narrowing.

It was true, Rifka had to put her husband and children first.

'Avi has work and we'll save money,' she told them. 'As soon as we have enough, we'll buy your tickets, and you'll join us.'

Fifteen years had passed before she sent the tickets for them to come.

Beneath the women's gallery the Schul is full of men. The air thickens with warm breath and prayer. The Ark is opened. The scrolls are clothed in white and gold. The men sway and sing,

Avinu Malkeinu

Our Father, our King, we have sinned before You,

Our Father our King, bless us with a good year....

She sways also and sings under her breath. As Avi says, there must be an explanation. Perhaps next year they'll come.

That night she sits for a long time alone in the kitchen before going upstairs.

Avi stirs when she sits on the edge of the bed. He opens his eyes, 'Are you alright?'

It isn't like him to even ask. She shrugs.

He reaches out and pats her arm, 'You worry too much.'

If only he would actually talk to her – sit up for once and look interested. Then she could finally say how she's really felt all these years – but he just squeezes her arm, and then flops back on the pillow.

She gets up and pulls back the curtain of their bedroom window. The moon shines down on the embankment, the river, and the sorrel.

She throws a shawl around her shoulders and goes downstairs. The stove still gives out some warmth. The smell from the chicken soup lingers in the kitchen.

She sits at the table and gazes at the flickering Jahrzeit candle. The kitchen door opens. It's Yitzhak, one of the workers. She pulls her shawl around her nightgown.

'I heard what happened, Rifka,' he says. 'It was the same thing with my mother and sister. At the last minute, they lost the courage to travel alone. So, we had to try again, and get someone to escort them. Now they're safe with my uncle in Manchester.'

Rifka sees immediately that this is the most likely explanation. Mama is sixty already, it was too much to expect that she and Leah should travel with strangers.

'Thank you,' she says to Yitzhak and smiles.

She will write to Mama and Leah and say she understands. She will send more tickets and find a cousin, or friend of a cousin to escort them. They can join the next group leaving from Kobrin.

Sadie gets a job in a detective agency and Rosa sells her ice skates. They both give Rifka money. Sol gives her all his wages, and Eli sends money from the fairground. Avi gives her extra housekeeping. She'll soon have enough money. She must make arrangements.

At Tu Bishvat, she comes home from the market, arms straining under the weight of her basket.

On the doormat, there's a letter with a Russian postmark.

Hope soars inside her, at last they've answered.

As usual, the Rabbi has written the address on the envelope but the letter inside isn't from Leah. It's from the Rabbi.

My dear Rifka,

I am sorry to tell you that there's been an outbreak of typhus. Your mother and Leah both got ill. We took the best care of them we could, but we couldn't save them. Their suffering was not too hard or long. They were both so excited about finally joining you in Wales. Their courage never faltered, but alas it was not to be. We have buried them in the cemetery, with many other of our community.

We will pray for you. Take comfort in your husband and children.

I send you my blessings and I wish you long life....

With trembling legs, she goes to the workshop. When she opens the door, everyone looks up and stops working.

'What is it?' Avi asks when he sees the expression on her face. He comes toward her. She hands him the letter. He reads it slowly.

He folds his arms around her. 'We will sit Shiva,' he says in a muffled voice.

She goes upstairs and turns her mirror to the wall. She finds a black shawl and covers her head. Somewhere, low stools are found for the family. Sadie and Rosa take over the cooking. In the evening, people gather. The Rabbi says prayers. Afterwards, the girls pass round tea and beigels with herring. News reaches Eli, and on the third night he comes home.

On the seventh night, after prayers, she's alone with Heime. He comes over, puts his hands on her head, and prays silently. Then he removes his hands and looks at her.

'We must mourn our loved ones,' he says, 'but death is part of life. Remember you have done your best. You have been a good wife and mother and you have been kind to me. Thankyou.'

Something softens inside her. When he leaves the room, she pulls the black shawl around her head more tightly.

She had tried to hide her shorn head from Mama, but one morning, going out to get firewood, she'd forgotten to put on her headscarf. 'Rifka!' Mama cried out when she saw her, 'what has happened to your beautiful hair?'

It was Mama who told Rifka they wanted a wet nurse at the big house. There were nerves in Rifka's stomach when she knocked at the back door. A delicious smell of roasting meat wafted towards her. She was allowed inside and went through the kitchen, passing an open fire where a pig roasted on a spit, fat splattering in the air. Her mouth watered at the sight of the forbidden meat. She followed the housekeeper up carpeted stairs to the nursery. The tall woman lifted the baby from its cradle and watched intently as Rifka took out her breast. She worried there wouldn't be enough milk left for Sol as the pale-faced creature tugged and sucked, but Mama had said that her body would produce what was needed. Later, the housekeeper gave her tea from a silver samovar – such a thing that her family could never dream of owning.

From her work as a wet nurse, and selling her hair, she had enough money for the land journey and the ship.

She had travelled with a group of other Jews, but they were strangers to her before she set out. On the second day, they came to a river with a narrow ford. The water was fast moving after the thaw. If you slipped, you could drown. Families helped each other wade across but Rifka was alone at the water's edge with Sol, a babe in arms, and Eli, a four-year-old child. She couldn't carry them both, couldn't leave either on the bank alone.

A woman she hadn't spoken to before had turned round to look at her from halfway across the river. She was carrying one child, and her husband, another. The woman spoke to her husband then shouted at Rifka, her voice carrying across the water, 'Wait there! My husband will come back for you.'

The man had come back and got them safely to the other side. She owed them her whole life, and that of her children, but she had never thanked them properly.

For Passover, the family gather around the table. Eli is with them. Nowadays he comes home often. Heime sits next to Avi as usual. Rifka feels closer to him than before. He tries to help them. Sometimes when Avi gambles, Heime stands outside the room, listening and frowning. She's heard him scolding Avi, and recently Avi did actually stop gambling for a couple of weeks. It isn't Heime's fault how things turned out with Mama and Leah.

Avi lifts the Seder plate and says, 'This is the bread of affliction which our fathers ate in the land of Egypt, All who are hungry come and eat.' Their ancestors left Egypt too quickly for the bread to rise. Bitter herbs are for suffering, and salt water for tears

She is still in mourning, but her family laugh and talk. The strain on the faces of the workers disappears as they drink the wine. Eli is telling a funny story. He enjoys entertaining people: a natural comedian, he could have gone on the stage. The story is about a Jewish boy who becomes a knight. The women chuckle, the men splutter and guffaw. Laughter spirals in the air.

She thinks of the opening words of the Passover service, 'All who are hungry, come and eat', not just a person's own family but all who are hungry. An idea comes to her, a way of making her life feel more worthwhile.

The next morning, she rises early and leaves Avi sleeping. On the way to the outhouse, she opens the door to the workshop and lets out the foul air. The men are still lying like dogs on the floor. Later when she gets home, she'll bring them coffee with extra sugar.

In the kitchen she lights the stove so there's warmth for the household. She makes tea and takes a piece of matzo.

She leaves the house and walks quickly along the embankment. The birds have been clamouring since early morning.

By the embankment, daffodils have started to bloom. They glow yellow in the pale morning light. In the summer when it gets warm, she'll persuade Avi to declare a holiday and take the whole household to Barry. The workers could do with a day out by the sea.

At the docks there's that same man coiling a rope.

'Hello bach – I haven't seen you for a while."

She smiles and moves on to her normal place, where the ship from Hamburg will dock. There are the people she's suspicious of. The Christian women, the Jewish-seeming men. The sun rises in a clear blue sky. The birds circle and screech. She pulls her shawl around her.

The ships are on the distant water. They approach slowly, and one docks near where she is standing. She pushes her way on board and makes for the lower deck. There's a group of Jews huddled together, their puchs wrapped around their meagre belongings, confused, and excited.

She was so poor when she left Russia and the journey had been so hard.

Eli had cried constantly from hunger and cold, the thaw had started but the mud just made the walking harder, and all-around snow still lay on the ground. With no papers she had to keep the children quiet when they crossed the borders. She had spoken to Eli sharply to keep him stumm. He stared at her, eyes full of resentment.

A man comes up to her, small, with red hair and a beard. Next to him are his wife, holding a baby, two little boys and an older girl.

'Is this ship going to America?' he asks.

'I doubt it.'

'But we have tickets for America.'

'Let me see.'

He shows her the ticket. She recognises the letters, though she can only read properly in Yiddish.

'This says "Cardiff": you've reached the end of your journey,' she says.

'But we've used all our savings on this ticket, we've been tricked,' the man tells her.

'I am sorry. The world is an evil place.'

'We have cousins in America. Here we have no one.'

Rifka knows what she's going to do, whether Avi likes it or not. This is what she has come for.

'It's alright, I can help you," she says, "come with me. My husband Avi will give you work."

'So how many people are you planning to bring here, Rifka?' Avi asks that night when she climbs into bed.

He has barely spoken to the new arrivals, but he hasn't been rude to them either or told them to leave.

'That's it for now until there's more space.'

'And what about money? They have nothing, I suppose, and we don't exactly have plenty of work.'

'I'm sure they can make themselves useful,' she lowers her voice, 'and now we don't have to feed Mama and Leah.'

'They're not our family, Rifka. They're not our responsibility.'

'They are Jews like us, and they are strangers in this land. Besides if you're so worried about money, why don't you finally stop gambling, like you keep promising your father?'

She looks down at her hands and waits for him to speak.

'It makes you feel better, to help people, doesn't it, Rifka?' he says after a while. His voice is gentle – thoughtful, almost. He doesn't sound angry.

'Yes.'

They look at each other.

'Alright,' he shrugs. 'If that's how you feel.'

'Thank you.'

She kisses his cheek. His beard is prickly. He kisses the top of her head and falls back on the pillow. Soon he's snoring.

In the morning, she'll wander down by the embankment. She'll pick daffodils for the table and try to find sorrel. Some time, in a month or a year, they'll have more space, or more work, and when that happens, she'll go back to the docks to fetch more people.

Sarah Lerner lives and works as a legal aid lawyer in the East End of London. She has recently trained as a mediator. Her short stories have been published by *Indie Novella* and *Jewish Fiction*, and have also been broadcast on Spanish-language radio. Her as yet unpublished novel, *Malaika*, was shortlisted for the Mslexia Novel Competition in 2024, and longlisted for the Exeter Novel Prize in 2023.

June 4th, 7.30pm - Book-ish, Crickhowell
June 5th, 12.30pm - BookHaus, Bristol
June 6th - Mr B's Emporium, Bath
July 3rd - Pen'rallt Gallery & Bookshop
July 4th - Awen Menai, Menai Bridge

BOUNDARY WATERS
TRISTAN HUGHES

BOUNDARY
WATERS

TRISTAN HUGH

'Sleek, savvy, scrupulous. This book is a triumph' – Abigail Parry

BREAKING A MAR
CHRISTINA THATCHE

pril 2nd, 6pm - Doylestown Bookshop, Pennsylvania, USA
pril 10th, 7pm - Waterstones Cardiff, 2A The Hayes
pril 16th, 7.30pm - Ye Olde Murenger House, Newport
pril 23rd, 7pm- The George Hotel, Devonshire St. Penrith
pril 24th, 6.30pm - The Farmer's Arms, Lowick Green, Ulverston
pril 26th, 4pm - Corner Stones Library, Gabriel Street, St Ives, Cornw
ay 11th, 7pm - Exmouth Arms, Bath Road, Cheltenham
une 7th, 2pm - Drawing Projects, 10 Stallard Street, Trowbridge
une 14th, 1pm - Storyville Books, Pontypridd

THIS ROOM IS IMPOSSIBLE TO EAT
Nicol Hochholczerová with Julia and Peter Sherwoo

May
6th, 6pm UCL, London
7th, 5pm Shulman Auditorium, Queen's College, Oxford
9th, 7pm Book-ish Crickhowell
10th, 5pm North Books, Hay-on-Wye
11th, 3.30pm Book Space, Cardiff
13th, 7pm Gloucester Road Books, Bristol
15th, 6.30pm Hatchards, the Strand, London

NICOL HOCHHOLCZEROV
TRANSLATED BY JULIA AND PETER SHERWOOD

THIS
ROOM IS
IMPOSSIBL
TO EAT

PITCH

KATHERINE STANSFIELD

OK, SO, HERE IT IS. LAST NIGHT ON TV (SOME KIND OF CULTURE show) I saw this executive producer talking about a new tv show she wants to make. It's going to be a tv show about people watching the people who are filmed watching tv in their own homes, sitting on the sofa talking to each other about the tv they are watching. You know the show. The original show. We've watched it, right here, on this sofa. So I had this idea. A great idea. You're going to love it. OK, here it is. Are you ready? My idea is that you and I audition to go on the new show watching people watching tv and talking to each other about it. We'll need to practise so the audition stands out because the exec said competition will be fierce. Because it's such a great idea, the new show. Very original. Very meta. Says something, doesn't it, about how we see the world. Layers.

How do you feel about this idea? Maybe you could verbalise that feeling, and just move over to the window, open the curtains. Get closer to the glass. Has Next Door got their curtains open as well? See, we're already practising being watched while we watch others! But proper practice will require the tv element, obviously. So, next step, we move the tv outside so Next Door can watch us watching the original show of people watching tv and talking about it, and we get some feedback from them. Or maybe we don't need to move the tv, just the sofa and then we watch the original show on my phone and talk about it. Let's put a pin in that for now. But the idea's good.

And once we've got a good audition clip, a really good one, we send it to the tv exec who will show it to the other execs (they all watch together) and they'll choose the stars of the new show, those who'll watch people watching tv. And the people watching tv will be watching new tv themselves. All new shows for this show about watching people watching people watching tv. So that's good. No risk of things being stale.

And to make our audition truly 'pop', I'm thinking we don't limit ourselves to just watching people watching people watching tv. Here me out: we keep it up when we turn off our tv. We don't stop. We watch each other when we go to sleep and carry on when we get up the next morning and shower, make toast. We watch each other carefully, deeply, and we talk about it. To ourselves at this stage, obviously, but we'll imagine the audience, because I know someone somewhere will see us, see our audition clip, and then the crew will come round to watch us on our sofa watching the tv show of people watching tv and talking to each other about it and then it won't be just you and I and the tv anymore. We'll have so much more to say to each other and won't that be great? Won't that make all of this worthwhile?

Katherine Stansfield is a multi-genre novelist and poet who grew up on Bodmin Moor and now lives in Cardiff. Her Cornish Mysteries alternative detective crime series is set in the 1840s. Katherine is also one half of the writing partnership DK Fields, with her partner David Towsey. Head of Zeus published all books in their political fantasy trilogy, the Tales of Fenest, the latest of which (*Farewell to the Liar*) was published in 2021.

LAST PAGE: TILTH

RHIANNON HOOSON ON AN EARTHY WORK IN PROGRESS

You and I are Earth, 1661

IN THE MUSEUM OF LONDON IS AN UNASSUMING PIECE OF CROCKERY which has become an unexpected object of fondness. It's a tin-glazed earthenware plate, emblazoned with the phrase 'You & i are Earth, 1661' in blue calligraphy. It was found in a sewer, and its maker remains, sadly, unknown. Part memento mori, part plate-based pun, part moment of connection with nature, I found it compelling from the moment I saw it. For a memento mori, it was curiously companionable, almost comforting – rather than returning to dust, we were already a part of the earth, and what's more, we were there together.

The Spoilheaps

My interesting fact of choice in case of unexpected icebreaking exercises: my first word was mud. I was a child that grew up in the mud, always digging in the garden, or making mud pies and potions, or stamping in the puddles in my red wellies. My dad was an archaeologist who knew the hills and their dead. The track behind our house was hollowed out on one side and you could see the layers of clay and rock in it. They felt different to the touch, in various pleasing ways.

Now I live under a hill bisected by the border. Radnorshire is no rich farming country like Herefordshire next door. What soil we have has blown in and halfway blown out again, at least on the hilltops. You can stand on the top of Stonewall Hill, in a field of fresh ploughed earth that has dried grey under your boots, and look down into Herefordshire, the whole brimming saucer of it, where the orchards are budding and the bare corduroy fields are red as blood. This small massif, a world in miniature, was a source of inspiration for me during lockdown, when I walked it extensively. It formed the basis for an essay of nature writing that never quite seemed ready to be put away. Eventually I hit on a rough idea for something bigger.

Tilth would be a book of landscape writing that would use my hill as a lens for an exploration of our relationship with the earth. Soil as an endangered resource. Soil as a nation in and of itself and soil as a part of our national identity. Earth as a source of pigments and the art that has emerged from it over the ages. Things buried, and things unearthed. Things forgotten, and things recorded in the soil itself. A personal record of a year on the hill, and the solace to be found in the nature, history and folklore there, but also a deep dive into the ground itself.

Terra Firma/ Terra Incognita
Things shift, and the hill moved under me: I became ill and never got better. I couldn't walk the hill anymore like I used to. Sometimes I couldn't even see it. Even though it loomed over me, I felt a dry sort of grief for it. Where before I would compose work on a morning walk there, now there seemed always to be glass between me and the hill.

I studied maps in obsessive detail, tracking mutating names (Llys-y-wern became Leysevern) and roads that became tracks that became bracken-filled footpaths. The hill was shifting again, becoming something not quite so fixed in the present, still marked with the roads of abandoned villages and even, on the sheltered side, pleasure gardens that later became pigsties. The hill came back piecemeal, not in organised chapters but in poems that grew through the project like mycelia.

Where before I had envisioned a nonfiction book that tracked a year through soil and its complexities, what has been slowly taking shape is a hybrid book that mixes landscape writing and poetry, dipping into history and the voices of those that might once have inhabited the hill. It matters less now that I've never been able to walk the footpath with the chainsawed finger post, where the bodies of dead moles hang like dried little mummies along the fence. It matters less that when I do get up there, I don't cover miles, striding dauntless and tireless and alone, but walk in smaller bursts, stopping to view a more intimate landscape.

Tilth is coming quietly, stranger than I'd thought, more a thing of the borderlands, but still with its feet mired in the mud – which can only be a good thing.

Rhiannon Hooson is a Welsh poet, author, and editor. She has won major awards for her work, including an Eric Gregory award from the Society of Authors. Her first book, *The Other City*, was a finalist for the Wales Book of the Year award and her long-form essay set on the Welsh borders, 'Archipelago', was highly commended in the New Welsh Writing Awards Rheidol Prize for Prose with a Welsh Theme or Setting in 2021. She has performed at literature festivals across the UK and in Europe, and her work has been featured in publications including *New Welsh Review/Reader*, *The Guardian*, *Magma*, and *Poetry Wales*. In the past few years, she has been a Literature Wales bursary recipient, writer in residence at the Hay Festival, winner of the First Chapter Award, and judge of the PENfro festival poetry competition. Rhiannon has a PhD in poetry from the University of Lancaster, where she taught creative writing, and has spent time living and working in Cumbria and Mongolia before settling in the Welsh marches. Her latest book, *Goliat*, was recently published by Seren. Her hybrid book of landscape writing and poetry, *Tilth*, is forthcoming.